HOTEL BARS AND LOBBIES

Hotel
BARS and LOBBIES

Carol Berens

McGraw-Hill
New York   San Francisco   Washington, D.C.   Auckland   Bogotá
Caracas   Lisbon   London   Madrid   Mexico City   Milan
Montreal   New Delhi   San Juan   Singapore
Sydney   Tokyo   Toronto

Library of Congress Cataloging-in-Publication Data

Berens, Carol.
    Hotel bars and lobbies / Carol Berens.
       p.   cm.
    ISBN 0-07-005828-8 (hardcover)
    1. Hotel lobbies. 2. Bars (Drinking establishments) I. Title.
  NA7800.B45 1996
  728'.5—dc20   96-1054
                                        CIP

McGraw-Hill

A Division of The McGraw·Hill Companies

1 2 3 4 5 6 7 8 9 0 11MP/11MP 9 0 1 0 9 8 7 6

ISBN 0-07-005828-8

The sponsoring editor for this book was Wendy Lochner, the editing
supervisor was Penny Linskey, and the production supervisor
was Pamela Pelton. Interior design and composition: Silvers Design

Printed and bound by Printvision.

McGraw-Hill books are available at special quantity discounts to use as premiums
and sales promotions, or for use in corporate training programs. For more information,
please write to the Director of Special Sales, McGraw-Hill, 11 West 19th Street,
New York, NY 10011. Or contact your local bookstore.

This book is printed on acid-free paper.

To F.J. and S.J.P.B.

CONTENTS

FOREWORD

Here they all are: those grand public spaces that permit us to live like royalty. Sumptuous palaces were once the stuff of royal privilege, open to only an invited few. But now they are public, and their dazzling splendor is available by appointment or whim. In the nineteenth century America led the way, creating hotels of such luxury and grandeur that Europeans were amazed. Since then, every country has gotten into the business of making comfort accessible, offering Western amenities around the globe.

The aesthetic range of these interiors is startling, from contemporary minimalism to fin de siècle excess. None offers a commonplace setting from everyday events, each forms a public stage to act out the stuff of dreams. Grand living rooms, urban resorts, designer visions: all are to be found and enjoyed in these pages.

The rooms resonate with civility. They could only occur in cities. Here they form an integral part of what defines urban character. Always the social heart of their communities, each has earned the privilege of evoking fond memories. Who could imagine a true city without one? Like the great plazas and parks of each urban place, these hotels celebrate opportunities for people to come together. They are a welcoming presence, inviting and appealing to all.

So are the bars. These are not hideaways to escape social encounter, they encourage it, using every possible design device to make their patrons feel and look good. These bars also come in all sizes, shapes, and aesthetic distinction. They give refuge and comfort. They offer balm, not oblivion. Even if it's temporary, these watering holes give patrons a sense of well-being found nowhere else.

Everyone will find a favorite place recorded here. And interspersed with present images are those of long ago; places which still beckon, although vanished into memory. For instance, some of us find the clock at New York's Biltmore Hotel just as real as ever, and many of the meetings it fostered remain fresh. True, the hotel where it once hung has vanished, but now we have this splendid book to make certain such memories remain bright.

Hugh Hardy

ACKNOWLEDGMENTS

I am indebted to many who had faith in my venture. For his spirited support and imaginative spark that turned the designers' instinct—criticism—into a constructive endeavor, I am forever grateful to Steve Diskin. Paula and Philip Forman were mainstays, their assured confidence an inexhaustible reserve from which I often drew. The encouragement and prodding of Henry Thomas eased the difficult effort of perseverance.

For their valuable comments and suggestions on my manuscript, I thank Judith Bing and Patricia Zedalis. Anne Asher and Leah Madrid listened to me with willingness and endless patience. I extend my sincere gratitude to James Stewart Polshek, Frank Israel, and Laurie Beckelman for reading proposals and drafts and then putting their thoughts to paper.

My travels around the country would have been much less enjoyable and productive without the warmth, welcome, and directional guidance of the Tinuccis, Deborah and Ralph Mitzenmacher, and Jean Stringer. Overseas, Patricia Bungener, Patrick Weiler, Caroline Hatt, Jean-Francois Kindermans, and Dick and Jacqueline Loehr played the hosts, guides, and translators in my explorations.

Last, but not least, my spirits were greatly buoyed by the support and interest of my colleagues at work who never tired of asking after my progress and who eagerly shared the fruits of their research.

For their extra efforts I would like to thank: Tom Pflueger of John M. Pflueger Architect AIA; Morris Lapidus; Michelle Saevke of the Westin St. Francis; Samara Zuwaylif of the Sheraton Palace Hotel; Timothy F. Nugent of the Governor Hotel; Ken Price of the Palmer House Hilton; Judith Bond and Nancy J. Weisinger of the Hotel Del Coronado; Kenneth Caldwell of ELS/Elbasani & Logan Architects; David Beer of Brennan Beer Gorman/Architects, Tim Samuelson and Richard Rauh.

I am indebted to all of those individuals, institutions; and hotels that helped me with photographs and permissions including: The Adolphus (David M.

Davis II); The Algonquin Hotel (Barbara McGurn); Architectural Record (Carolyn Koenig); Arizona Biltmore (Laura L. Jordan); Avery Architectural and Fine Arts Library, Columbia University in the City of New York; Atlanta Marriott Marquis (Sandy Huff); Bel-Air Hotel (Carol Ann Kelly); The Benson Hotel (Robert J. Parson); The Beverly Hills Hotel (Terri Dishman); Brown Palace Hotel (Emily Schmid); Brown's Hotel (Valerie Marshall); Cairo Marriott (Sarah Simon); Capital Hotel (Karen Lafferty/Edwin B. Cromwell); Chicago Architectural Photographing Company/David R. Phillips; Chicago Historical Society; Cincinnati Historical Society; Claridge's (Catherine Robinson); Clift Hotel (Donna Hall); Coral Gables Biltmore (Sherry Miller Reinker); Culver Pictures; The Dorchester (Martine de Geus); The Fairmont Hotel (Cynthia Bowman); Four Seasons Hotel, New York (Rebecca Werner); Four Seasons Olympic Hotel, Seattle (Elaine Griffin); Grand Hyatt-Hong Kong (Hyatt International, Lisa Smith); Heathman Hotel (Darlene Frahm); Henry Holt and Company, Inc. (Mimi Ross); Hotel Alfonso XIII (Belen Mann); Hotel Angleterre (Anne Brogaard); Hotel Atop Bellevue (Suzanne Shissler/Simon Public Relations Group); Hotel Daneli (Ugo Balaudo); Hotel Konig von Ungarn (Christian Binder); Hotel Le Bristol (KWE Associates/Charles Mardiks); Hotel Montalembert (Valerie Legrand); Hotel Pera Palas (Leyla Taskin); Hôtel Plaza Athénée (Françoise Reboul); Hotel Ritz Madrid (Ana Soto); Hyatt Regency Atlanta (Carol Teacher); Hyde Park Hotel (Derrion Farrell); Imperial Hotel; Inn of the Anasazi (Angie Cross); Hotel Inter-Continental, Chicago (Carrie Lannon); The Jefferson (Mary Stuart Cruickshank); Los Angeles Biltmore (Maureen Stokes and Holly Barnhill); La Fonda Hotel (Lisa Bertelli); La Valencia (Audrey Steidl); Leading Hotels of the World (Kylie Robertson, Penny VanMaldeghem); Le Grand Hotel Inter-Continental (Corinne Guedj); Le Grand Hotel-Rome; London Ritz (Jenny Johnson); Lou Hammond Associates (Susan Bang, Wendy May); The Majestic (Ellie Kane); Mandarin Hotel; Manila Hotel (Annie D. Ringor); Mayfair Hotel (Deborah McLoughlin); Museum of the City of New York (Marguerite Lavin); New York Palace (Michele Spiceland/Zimmerman Agency); Hotel Nikko Beverly Hills (Dianne Briskin); Oriental Bangkok; Oxford Hotel (Tito Christensen); Palace Hotel-Madrid (Carmen Castro); Paramount Hotel (Tracy Spencer-Wright/Nancy Assuncao Associates); Park Lane London (Rose Clayton); Le Parker Meridian (Rose Genovese); Peabody Hotel (Gentry Brown); Peninsula Hotel (Nerissa Roselada/Murphy O'Brien Communications); Pfister Hotel (Neil Salerno/Sandra H. Spann, Ellingesen/Sprecher); Pierre Hotel (Mary Jo McNally); Regent Hotel-Hong Kong (Janice Lam); Rockwell Group (Joan MacKeith); Royalton Hotel (Nadia Donato); Sacher Hotel (Erna Koprax); Savoy Hotel (Pamela Carter); Seelbach Hotel (Viola Sanders); Shangri-La Hotels (Marion Darby); Sorrento Hotel (Eileen Mintz); St. Regis Hotel (Eleanor Lambert Ltd); Turner Entertainment Co. (Kathy Lendech); Williard Inter-Continental Hotel (Ann McCracken).

LOBBIES, BARS, AND SPECIAL ROOMS

The main entrance…should be regarded as of great importance, as it is the heart
of the building from which all life springs and to which it returns.
Henry Janeway Hardenbergh

Lobbies impress, greet, and disperse arrivals and, nowadays, usually secure the rest of the building. Most entries exist solely to be passed through, anterooms to the main event beyond. They tell us something about the building, as efficiently or as elaborately as the owner decrees, and then guide us to our intended destination. The office building lobby can be quite an elegant and active place, but no matter how rich the materials or vast the space, they remain corridors to be traversed. Even the apartment building lobby, despite the usual living room seating provided, is a place in which to spend as little time as possible.

The hotel lobby is different. To be successful, it must do all the impressing, greeting, dispersing, and securing the office or apartment building. It is, however, a destination in itself. Its sure sense of place combined with wonder and glamour intrigues and beguiles.

The hotel lobbies and special rooms explored in this book make a statement as they welcome and delight. Public in nature, they generate a sense of arrival, socially as well as physically. Yet, in reality and in our imaginations, they evolve into our private reserves. They are comfortable places to enjoy, to claim as our own, or to share with others. They are our public living rooms where we can join friends or business acquaintances for a drink or for an evening's entertainment.

Lobbies are where our public and private worlds meet. The fragile balance between openness and exclusivity is at the core of good lobby design. This convergence and ambiguity enriches and smoothes the edges of urban life and allows us to participate in its urbaneness.

This sense of place is critical in present day America where locations for public life are fast disappearing. Europe has its cafe culture to serve as a mediating social institution. The United States, however, has no such pervasive tradition. Hotel lobbies and public rooms are among the few remaining places where public interaction is not only prized, it is expected.

Some hotels are so in tune with the life of the city around them that they become part of its public landscape and tradition. The very name of a hotel evokes the essence of its place and time. The clock in the now demolished New York Biltmore Hotel was immortalized as the meeting place of choice for F. Scott Fitzgerald's rich in love. Though long gone, this icon of the jazz era captured the imagination of a generation and this phenomenon continues. Just say "The Polo Lounge" to conjure up images of deals made and lost in the Beverly Hills Hotel and "Meet me under the clock" in San Francisco to rendezvous at the Westin St. Francis.

Identification with time and place is not the exclusive terrain of American hotels. Throughout the world hotel bars and lobbies become the center of activity for the international crowd, whether business people, expatriates of the moment, locals, or just curious travelers. Writers and public figures keep Raffles forever entwined with Singapore, the Mandarin Oriental with Hong Kong, and the Ritz with Paris.

In researching this book, I was struck by how reminiscences and incidental events comprise much of what is written about hotels. Volumes trace authors' grand tours to famous hotels around the world, complete with descriptions of whom they met, how friendly they became with the maitre d's and what unusual experiences they encountered. Asked about their favorite hotel, people more often than not recall fleeting, sometimes, poetic images and vague impressions— impressive flower arrangements, sunlight shimmering on walls, sounds of splashing water in a fountain, the dress of the patrons in the bar. The hotel experience is intensely personal and emotional, layered with importance and meaning not explicitly concerned with design. Why we like or respond to one place more than another is as ephemeral as the images evoked by memories: sounds, colors, service, social ambiance.

Indeed, hotels and their lobbies hold a sensitive place in our psyches because they translate the vague and amorphous images of what we admire and cherish into places we enjoy. To be successful, these rooms must embody our idea of the good life embedded in our cultural consciousness. In foreign countries, they connect us to the otherworldness of travel with its implicit possibilities of adventure and catered comfort.

Whether peering fearlessly into the future or luxuriating in visions of the past, hotel lobbies are an exploration of the complex, multi-leveled development of a design idea. We enter the hotel expectant and ready to be impressed or perhaps, even better, overwhelmed. A clear, definite image first strikes us. This unifying idea must be immediately and readily understood. It must maintain the balance between being easily recognizable and complex enough to be expandable and adaptable. Above all, it must never be ordinary, monotonous, or dull.

This is a total design environment. Details upon details reinforce and enhance the central idea. This layering can be seen throughout the procession of spaces, the thematic colors and materials as well as all the incidental specialties such as uniforms, glassware, swizzle sticks, and match books. Not only are we aware that such small details have been considered, we revel in that awareness.

The Urban Experience

One of the defining characteristics of urban life is that it is lived in public. There are times, however, when rampant urbanism must be tamed. The best respite from frenzied streets is the well-designed, well-tended hotel lobby. Here, one can find an attitude fast disappearing in the public realm—courtesy is respected and one's comfort is important. Here, telephone booths come equipped with shelves and note paper; restrooms are clean. Here, implicitly, one is safe.

Hotel lobbies and bars are an important civilizing element in the urban landscape. They greet and provide comfort for their own guests as well as welcome all (usually for a price). Their roles are as numerous and diverse as their clientele: a place to meet strangers or lovers, a comfortable setting to pass the awkward time between appointments, a clean restroom or just an air-conditioned stopover in a busy day.

The urban hotel lobby, as a mediator between our public and private worlds, is where the life lived in public is important. To see and be seen is the essence of urban style. Lobbies provide the backdrop for scenes of urban drama. People are primary. In some lobbies it is difficult to determine which demands more attention, the people or the decor. Indeed, effective designs endeavor to make the guests look good by creating spotlights of activity and complementary settings. These lobbies are dependent upon human activity and interaction for the design to come to life. Good design strives to create an atmosphere that encourages conversation, socializing, and the urban constant, serendipity.

This book explores the variety of urban hotel public rooms as they exist today and how they appeared in the past. The world is full of wonderful places; however, these lobbies, bars, and special rooms were selected for their whole-hearted embrace of the urban. Their public nature exerts a critical role in the life of their city, either in civilizing reality or in capturing and reflecting its collective imagination.

HOTEL BARS AND LOBBIES

Chapter 1

CREATING THE FANTASY

Suppose a director came to me with a script that called for a fabulous, luxurious tropical hotel setting. "Give it to me. Knock their eyes out with it. It has got to be fabulous." I'd say, "All right, I'll design a fabulous movie set." And that's what I did."
Morris Lapidus

HOTEL BARS and lobbies are those wonderful places where ordinary life enters the realm of high drama. Just as good theater creates its own world as it illuminates our real one, hotel bars and lobbies are the stages that reflect society's images of what it both values and finds extraordinary. While mirroring our collective visions of the good life, these rooms must also perform many different roles, naturally and with apparent ease.

Hotel bars and lobbies, more than any other form of architecture or interior design, are realized fantasies. Whether the quintessential setting for the urban rendezvous, the total-concept resort, the comfortable home away from home, or office away from office, lobby design has few equals in the demand for evoking a special character and atmosphere. Its image is its reality. Successful design creates an image that welcomes its guests as it imposes its exclusive personality, an image that declares its version of life as it is best lived.

To enter the hotel lobby is to walk onto a stage set and into a world of wonder and expectation. These lobbies and bars are decisively scripted, with plots ranging from urban sophistication and luxurious elegance through paneled clubbiness and rustic gentility. Each demands its own behavior and demeanor from us, who play the dual roles of spectators in the audience and actors on stage.

The most literal hotel fantasies today occur at Las Vegas and Atlantic City extravaganzas. Egyptian tombs, ancient Rome, and the wild west all compete for the gambler's dollar. The atmosphere and design of these large-scale amusement parks strive to overwhelm, a philosophy that meshes perfectly with these hotels' role as destinations. Their avid repeat customers are testament to their success.

The clock at New York's Biltmore Hotel (destroyed). (MCNY, The Byron Collection)

Their stated goal, however, is to extract large amounts of money from their patrons and not to encourage social interaction and discourse. They function more as retail spaces than hotel lobbies. For this reason, they are not treated in this book.

ROLES

As stage sets, lobbies and bars are backdrops for the human drama to unfold. How we look and feel and act in these lobbies are as critical to our enjoyment as the images they portray. Just as a play needs an audience to be enjoyed, lobbies rely on the energy of people and the sounds of conversation and ice against a glass to come alive. We do not pass through these rooms anonymously but engage in two roles simultaneously: actor and spectator. As active participants, we go to the lobby to be seen—posing and artifice are not unknown. The decor's job is to show us off to our best advantage. As spectators, we are the appreciative eyes of who and what are around us. The room must provide us with the best vantage points. Both roles are vital to the success of the lobby.

Skillfully designed lobbies demand something from us; they oblige us to react. Good design does not arouse neutrality. Since lobbies mirror our ideas of the good life, we must accept the reflection. If the design is too strong or personally conflicting, we feel imposed upon and uncomfortable. If we disapprove of unbridled luxury, an overgilded, overstuffed lobby offends. If our tastes adhere to the traditional, a cutting-edge design might threaten. If we prefer to be unobtrusive and anonymous, we recoil at a design that puts us on display.

The original lobby of Miami Beach's Fountainebleau Hotel by Morris Lapidus caught the imagination of 1950s vacationers as the perfect stage on which to play the leading role. This lobby captured the exuberance and flamboyance of its place and purpose. (Morris Lapidus, Architect)

STYLES AND IMAGE

The most popular version of life as it is best lived is the one that was lived in the past, if only in our mythological memories. Hotel lobbies evoke times and places few have experienced but whose images appeal clearly and directly to an accepted concept of elegance, an elegance that bespeaks of class, warmth, and personal attention. Thus, the cities of America are strewn with interpretations of Italian palazzi, French Renaissance chateaux, and English gentlemen's clubs while Spanish missions, southern mansions, and Moorish arches nestle in the countryside.

Cutting-edge design is rarely seen in hotel lobbies. When done well this design style creates exciting and visionary places, defining its own clear version of individualistic sophistication while not referring to other times or far-off places. More modern than today could ever be, it invents its own vocabulary and stakes out its own design frontier. Critical to cutting-edge design is the creation of a theme that will not grow old and tiresome before it is time for the first guests to check in.

Over the years, almost all regions and epochs have inspired hotel design. The International Style is an exception, however. Noted for its theoretical basis of good taste and lack of ornament, this style never became fashionable for hotel lobbies, perhaps because its cerebral style did not project the expected graciousness. Hotel patrons searching for warmth and fantasy were greeted instead with hard lines and truthful design. Considered cold and functional, the International Style suggests another prosaic day at the office rather than an excursion to wonderland.

Ironically, the inheritors of the International Style's call for spare and simple lines are the standard, anonymous airport or chain hotels. Perhaps with a bit more applied detail, flowered carpets, and ersatz materials than Mies van der Rohe would have envisioned or condoned, these hotels command a simple and direct approach toward their function. Exemplifying the belief that modern connotes cleanliness and efficiency, these hotels have made their mark as the low-frill, always reliable option for travelers seeking accommodations, not aesthetic or social sustenance.

How accurately an image coincides with our ideals of the elegant or the exceptional is the measure of a lobby's success. Whether details are true or authentic is immaterial and incidental to our enjoyment. As with set designers adept at producing illusions, lobby designers create live-in, walk-on stages that convey the essence of an era, style, or social tone. Stage sets present images of authenticity by not duplicating reality. Flats represent three-dimensional objects, and false perspective portrays distance. In fact, real objects often appear out of place and out of scale on the stage.

Shameless appropriation and manipulation of other times and other cultures are the hotel designer's forte. Taking stylistic liberties is not a modern phenomenon; it has long been a hallmark of lobby design. Design explorations of exotic and fantasy locations abound, although never superseding old-world elegance as the most desired style.

At the turn of the century, the illusion of traveling around the globe within the perimeter of a city block became the rage. Perhaps influenced by the 1893 Chicago World's Columbian Exposition, which whetted America's curiosity of things foreign, images of other countries became a source of inspiration and entertainment. With the spirit of trying on new costumes for a high school play, Americans threw themselves into experiencing the trappings of other lands, if only for tea or dinner. (Perhaps not surprisingly, these images never recalled the countries or conditions that resulted in the massive waves of arriving immigrants.)

Some hotels pursued variety as a major marketing objective. The Hotel Astor (1904 and 1910) unabashedly contained every style and even invented a few. As a contemporary review stated:

> There are French rooms, which are extremely French, German rooms which are desperately German, Dutch rooms which are fearfully Dutch, a Pompeian room which makes one think of Vesuvius, Chinese and Japanese rooms which are as Oriental as a Buddhist god, a yachting cabin and a hunting lodge for convivial sailors and shooters, and finally, several rooms in the "new art" style, which are about the most extraordinary things in the whole extraordinary collection.[1]

Impressions of exotica, not authenticity, hold sway. Nowhere was the concept that illusion supplants reality given freer rein than at the Miami Beach hotels of Morris Lapidus. During the design of the Fountainebleau, when faced with a client who wanted "...not that old-fashioned French Provincial...[but] that nice modern French Provincial,"[2] the architect responded with energy and élan. To the joy of vacationers and the distress of architectural critics, his glamour referred not to France, nor indeed to the provinces of any known country. Fluted illumi-

nated columns, patterned marble floors, and lots of glass chandeliers along with undulating surfaces and round forms all screamed "French" under the hot Miami sun.

Reflecting other cultures through fantasy and impressionistic images is not an exclusive American trait. The design of westernized outposts in North Africa and Asia stylizes what is just beyond their front doors. These abstractions, combined with foreign (that is, western) design, create their own exotic allure, dual fantasies conjuring up imaginary places that exist nowhere except in the lobbies themselves. Western and local images are equally synthetic and approximate. Maintaining a safe refuge for westerners allows the host country to be viewed from afar, from public rooms that express just enough local character to convince travelers they are no longer in Ohio or Lille.

No matter where it is located, however, a good urban hotel's sense of theater, and thus its identity, prevails. Traveler or native can both be carried away by images of other worlds and the adventures that hotel lobbies and bars convey. Its stage is set; its show goes on.

Chapter 2

MAKING AN ENTRANCE

THE ENTRANCE of a good urban hotel is plainly visible; finding it is not a problem. Flags, canopies, steps signal the way; valets and doormen with whistles hailing cabs do the rest. The hotel's command of the street expresses its embrace or disdain of its surroundings. The relationship and progression from the street, through the entrance, and to the lobby reflect its concept of its civic nature.

Hotel entrances waver between offering a gracious welcome and conveying subtle aloofness, between hospitality and exclusivity. Some hotel corridors are as public as the streets. At others, barriers—both architectural and human—foster an aura of elitism. Hotels' blank street walls or locked doors express ambivalence with the urban landscape at their doorsteps. Automobile and parking access further complicates and congests entrances. In addition, inept design can create the impression that how one gets to the lobby from the street has not been considered at all.

The success of a hotel lobby depends on the separation of public from private areas. The design question is how this separation is done, not whether it is done. Symbols demarcate the outside world from the hotel world, creating special places and allowing patrons and casual visitors to feel comfortable and secure. The raising of a curtain or the dimming of the lights signals the start of a play; a lobby needs such a devise to allow its story to begin. When differentiation is ignored, neither public nor hotel needs are fulfilled.

Traditional center-city hotel entrances relate directly to their surroundings. The building is easily identifiable; doors open right onto the street, under canopies raised in greeting. The lobby is just inside, often in direct view. This is

(Clift Hotel, San Francisco)

7

clearly demonstrated at New York's Plaza Hotel. Seen from a distance, the hotel presides over Grand Army Plaza: A public park is its front yard. It is its own landmark. There is no confusion about where one is. All activity centers at its entry: Pedestrians, automobiles, and even horse-drawn carriages all gather; the lobby and all its services are directly beyond the steps.

Blurring the distinctions between public and private occurred at Le Parker Meridien Hotel in New York. In order to build eight stories more than the thirty-two permitted under the zoning regulation, the hotel owners agreed to use its lobby as a public space, providing tables and chairs as amenities. But the Renaissance-inspired marbled atrium became, according to the hotel owners, a haven for thieves who would threaten and harass guests. The hotel removed the chairs and tables, reducing the atrium to a walk-through space. After several administrative hearings, city authorities required the chairs and tables to be

replaced in accordance with the development agreement. No law, however, can legislate how people will use the space.

A particularly comfortable entrance form is the *piano nobile,* which Chicago hotels adopted as their own. The traditional Chicago hotel lobby is located on the second floor. Perhaps as a shelter from blustery winter winds, an urban arcade connecting two or more streets occupies the ground floor and contains stores and services available to the general public as well as hotel guests. The arcade affirms the hotel's connection to the city as its lobby rises above it.

The Palmer House Hilton's elegant marble and glass arcade which connects three streets, including the main entrance, graciously fulfills a mediating role. The arcade's barbers, florists, and other retail shops comprising the ground floor also have street frontage, thereby further knitting the hotel into the fabric of the city.

The entrance to the Paramount Hotel in New York is sweet anonymity: fresh roses in lieu of flags or canopies (or even a sign). Flush glass doors fill existing masonry arches and convey modernity inserted within the old, which indeed represents the hotel's design. (Tom Vack/Paramount Hotel)

From the main entrance on Monroe Street, a grand staircase leads to a most spectacularly extravagant and ornate room. Coming on the lobby from below elicits a sense of movement and extra drama, more theatricality than entering the room directly from the same level. (Unfortunately, two ill-conceived escalators added at the opposite end of the room aesthetically clash with the lobby and diminish the experience of rising toward this main event.) The Drake Hotel and the Chicago Hilton (formerly the Stevens Hotel) also follow this design to great advantage, both for the hotel and for the city.

Unfortunately, after showing how to ingeniously integrate a hotel into its urban surroundings, Chicago has embraced the latest antiurban manifestation: the hotel located in a center-city high-rise, mixed-use mall. Both the Ritz-Carlton, Chicago, and the Chicago Four Seasons are on upper floors, sandwiched between a shopping mall below and offices and condominium apartments above. Reversing the

Chicago prototype, elaborate public entrances lead to retail uses, illustrating the hotels' abrogation of their civic presence. In both cases, a small elevator lobby acts as the hotel's entrance vestibule, its size constraining any sense of pomp and arrival. It is indeed a very determined soul who ventures into one of these hotels without a specific purpose. Which, perhaps, may be the whole point.

Separating entrance and lobby reduces street-level entrances to mere passageways with receptionists guarding the gates. This form, however, plays havoc with the hotel's most important design element. Majesty and importance require high ceilings and large volumes. Two-, three-, and even four-story ceiling heights bestow a sense of arrival and public welcome; the vastness of the space conveys prestige and authority to its patrons and guests. Contrasting and manipulating ceiling heights are some of the most dynamic and theatrical methods hotels have of impressing. Lacking this volume (either on the street or upstairs in the lobby

(Above) The Plaza presides over New York's famous outdoor room, the Grand Army Plaza.
(Carol Berens)

(Right) Is it public or is it private? The lobby of Le Parker Meridien in midtown New York, albeit beautifully designed and detailed, confused the roles. (Parker Meridien)

itself) the design must, with secondary means such as rich materials, convey elegance and distract the visitor from sensing that, for all this work, the ceiling is too low.

Relegated to simple waiting rooms, these small street foyers limit hotel access and contain nothing to encourage or sustain social interaction. The hotel's street presence is subdued. To compensate for this vacuum, the Four Seasons installed a sidewalk metal sculpture of a harried man trying to hail a cab in the rain. The sculpture, however humorous, only highlights the absence of more interesting human activity.

The most problematic entry of all occurs at atrium hotels whose lobbies always seem to be perched atop blank-walled podiums. Unfortunately, this is not just a bad design solution but is inherent in the building type itself and the hotel's requirement for large meeting rooms, ballrooms, and perhaps, parking. In traditional hotels, these large-span rooms are either located on the same floor as the main lobby or directly above it. In atrium hotels, however, this space is occupied by the atrium itself. Its floor plates are only the depth of perimeter guest rooms, and their centers are hollow. Therefore, these large function rooms can only be

(Top) New York's Marriott Marquis: Despite strings of lights attempting to mimic the spirit of its theater-district neighbors, the actual entrance to the hotel looks, smells, and sounds like a parking garage. (Carol Berens)

(Left) In cases of vehicular-pedestrian conflict, both the city and hotel guests are the losers. New York's Marriott Marquis's main entrance is actually in midblock, accessed through a tunnel underneath its building. Its entrance is very difficult to find, almost repelling guests. While actually extending a full city block on Broadway in the heart of Times Square, only a small sign with an arrow signals the main entrance. (Carol Berens)

accommodated at the building's base, thereby severing the lobby from the street. The more function rooms there are, the higher the base and the greater the separation. For instance, in New York, the Marriott Marquis's lobby is actually eight stories above Times Square.

Car-pedestrian conflicts often mar hotel main entrances, which at times can appear as frantic as a genie serving two masters. Frenzied confusion often results when center-city hotels accommodate these divergent needs. At large hotels, vehicular activity can overwhelm those entering on foot, leaving them unattended orphans at the door. Off-street vehicular drop-off requirements of newer hotels address the issue of street congestion but often result in both the urban fabric and the hotel's pride of entry losing in the bargain.

New York's Marriott Marquis: On a side street, a large semi-circular "canopy" indicates the driveway, which is not the service entrance, despite appearances, but the entrance to the hotel, whose eighth-floor lobby is only reachable by elevator. (Carol Berens)

The most common solution appropriates the form of the ceremonial entrance driveway but inserts it within the ground floor of a building. By setting buildings grandly back from the street, curved vehicular drives create wonderfully generous entrances and an impressive sense of arrival. In tight urban environments, however, these drives do not set off their buildings; the buildings swallow up the drives, as can be seen in the newer San Francisco hotels. The hotel then either has two entrances—one at the street and the other by the drive—or a single entrance, which by necessity has been relocated deep within the center of the building, unseen from the street. When approached on foot, the hotel is entered through dark passageways reminiscent of eerie parking garages rather than country estates.

The Los Angeles Biltmore resolved this dichotomy with aplomb. Its separate street and automobile entrances both lead to common areas in the interior. The vehicular entrance, in the new tower on Grand Street, leads to the registration desk and lobby. The lobby, in turn, opens up to the main galleria which connects Fifth and Sixth Streets, where traditional urban street entrances remain. On Olive Street, taking advantage of the change in street elevations, the Rendezvous Court, one story below, is reached directly from the street. Thus, there is a great sense of entry whether one enters by car or on foot. More important, the car entry does not preclude or override the hotel's street presence.

(Left) The original driveway entrance to San Francisco's Hyatt Regency (euphemistically dubbed a porte-cochère) effectively blocked the hotel from the streetscape. This area has recently been redesigned. (ELS/Elbasani & Logan Architects)

(Below) San Francisco's Hyatt Regency: The actual hotel entrance, by comparison, made the street facade look inviting. The entrance had been reduced to a driveway, where guests were deposited at the door as if at a garage. (ELS/Elbasani & Logan Architects)

(Far Right) The Biltmore, Los Angeles: The dramatic entrance on Olive Street proudly proclaims the hotel's urban presence. This entrance leads to the promenade which connects all the public rooms of the hotel. Vehicular entry is at the opposite, shorter axis. The arched entry of this restrained Beaux-Arts classical building echoes the arched storefront openings along the sidewalk, further integrating the hotel with its surroundings. (The Biltmore, Los Angeles)

The 1897 Waldorf-Astoria Peacock Alley's immense scale and classical detailing impressively set the tone of material extravagance that represented New York's upper class social life. The great number of service people at the ever-ready ensured that all needs and whims would be attended to at a moment's notice. (MCNY, Wide World Photos)

(Above) Today, the Willard Inter-Continental's Peacock Alley still connects its main lobby with the F Street lobby, with several function rooms in between. This classically inspired corridor was obviously not designed for a mere casual stroll. *(Willard Inter-Continental)*

(Right) Royal in materials, detailing, and color, the main entrance stair sets the tone for the Imperial Hotel, Vienna, Austria. *(Imperial Hotel)*

(Above) The grand stair dominates the
Jefferson Hotel's Rotunda in Richmond,
Virginia. (©1993 Prakash Patel/Jefferson Hotel)

(Right) An enlarged Piranesi print serves as
backdrop for the stair that went to nowhere
in the 1954 Fountainebleau Hotel in Miami
Beach. (Morris Lapidus)

THE PROMENADE: PEACOCK ALLEYS AND GRAND STAIRCASES

The hotel lobby is a stage set where everyone has a walk-on role. The promenade is its critical design feature; the procession is the essence of its experience. Whether to show off (as actor) or to walk through magnificent space and observe (as spectator), the promenade encourages human drama.

People have always paraded and strutted. It was the architect Henry Janeway Hardenbergh, however, who provided a special place for these performances. He is credited with creating a passageway so dramatic and so intensely used for showing off that it was immediately dubbed Peacock Alley. Located in the first Waldorf-Astoria Hotel (replaced in 1929 by the Empire State Building), this hall captured New York society's imagination, becoming the setting of its dynamic social urban scene.

Eight years later, this feature was again used by the same architect in the Willard Hotel (now the Willard Inter-Continental) in Washington, D.C., a city

where seeing and being seen define political and social life. This block-long promenade extends the length of the hotel from the main lobby to the F Street Lobby, ensuring that maximum exposure is achieved.

The most dramatic settings for the promenade are reserved for the grand staircase. From images of royal receptions to Hollywood chorines dancing up and down the steps, the stair elicits many symbols and meanings. Adaptable to any design theme, stairs represent the grandeur of ascent, the possibility for everyone to make sweeping entrances and exits.

The theatrical limits of the grand staircase reached their highest level with the Paris Opera House by Jean-Louis-Charles Garnier. Designed for unabashed self-display, its staircase posed the searing social question, "Which performance was more important, the one on the stage or the one in the lobby?" With this stair, hotel lobby design definitively changed. Although ceremonial stairs had long been central features of private palaces, it took the Opera stair for designers on both sides of the Atlantic to exploit the stair's dramatic public possibilities.

The hotel stair has both inspired and borrowed theatrical allusions. The staircase in the Jefferson Hotel in Richmond is said to be the model for Tara's in *Gone with the Wind*. And, on a less serious note, who cannot smile when seeing Hollywood step off the screen and materialize into the curving staircase of Miami Beach's Fountainebleau Hotel? The Fountainebleau actually served as a stage set for several scenes in *Goldfinger* with nary an adjustment. Its staircase, in fact, was created just for image and drama. Its notoriety exists not only because of its aggressive shape but because it was designed to convey an image. It leads nowhere.

The function of stairs is best summed up by Morris Lapidus: "You walk out. You see everybody. Everybody sees you. You are dressed in your best bib and tucker. Your neighbor is there. He sees that you are at the Fountainebleau. It's straight showmanship. I put those people on stage and they love it."[1] Few would disagree.

Chapter 3

THE AMERICAN PAST

One is verily tempted to ask if the hotel-spirit may not just be the American spirit most seeking and finding itself.
Henry James

DEMOCRACY AND ELEGANCE

T HE STORY of the rise of the hotel's prominent urban role is an American one—one which directly corresponds to the desires of a mobile, enterprising populace and incipient towns striving to establish reputations as cosmopolitan centers. It is a story of urban pride and civic breast-beating, as America's middle class appropriated symbols of the upper class. The social history of America can be read in the design of its hotels and their position in cities—the desire to outdo what was done before and the optimistic embrace of the newest, the biggest, the most exotic.

The American hotel as we know it developed when, in the early 1800s, the local inn or tavern expanded its public presence to serve a wider clientele than just travelers and wayfarers. Accommodating permanent residents as well as visitors, the hotel began providing fine dining rooms, reading rooms, libraries, meeting rooms, and expanded services, inaugurating its position as a center for cultural and communal activities. This new civic role transformed American hotels from small private institutions into social stages, their lobbies and public rooms open to all who could pay the price.

During the last decades of the 1800s and the first three of the 1900s, America saw fierce competition as hotels were built in reaction to others, each trying to outdo the others in size, elegance, or status. Symbolizing ambition and prosperity for emerging and growing metropolises, hotels helped remodel small urban centers into urbane trading and commercial hubs. Within cities, hotel development redefined or reinforced metropolitan growth patterns and prestige as expansion created new and more elegant districts. In so doing, these hotels became the focal points of civic and social activities. Their banquet halls were the

The lobby of the Congress Hotel was a famous (notorious) political center in Chicago in the early 1900s. Designed by Holabird and Roche in 1893, the lobby's heavy, solid appearance still seems to reek of deal-makers' cigars.
(Chicago Historical Society ICHI-15611)

locations of celebratory dinners, and their bars and restaurants became the sites of political and business deals and, of course, social drama.

Neither understated charm nor restrictive design comprised the vocabulary of these merchants, city shapers, and parvenus. This new middle class demanded big and bold. The main hotel in town often rivaled and surpassed public buildings in stylistic impressiveness as well as in the services it provided. Competing with the majesty of the new Capitol Building in Washington, these early hotels were often topped with rotundas. Soaring lobbies and great halls became commonplace. Before there were public libraries in some towns, hotel reading rooms offered news from around the country and acted as lending libraries.

These hotels catered to the populace as a whole and to a new middle class in particular. Its desire to clothe itself in the trappings of the upper class reflected the belief that refinement and glamour were available to all. This "democratization of elegance," as Henry James disparagingly described it in the early 1870s, broadened the appeal of these hotels and reflected a growing fluidity in American society. In Europe, class as manifested in the grand hotels was restrictive; in America, these symbols, at least, were appropriated and made potentially attainable.

In the nineteenth century, American hotels played such a strong role in the social, political, and business life of cities and burgeoning towns that it was the rare foreign commentator who resisted seeing them as metaphors of the American character. Openness, crassness, friendliness, and the ease of mixing business with pleasure were all traits of the collective American personality said to be exhibited in the use of hotels, public rooms, and lobbies.

As with all unknown or exotic cultures, foreigners in the 1800s compared America with what they knew, remarking on similarities and differences. The Trollopes (first Mrs. Frances Trollope, then her son, Anthony) and Charles Dickens were among the English who observed the august physical presence of American hotels that overshadowed civic structures. This confusion of roles was understandable when classical and formal hotel designs incorporated granite and marble columns and rotundas to create rather somber, imposing buildings. In 1847, D. F. Sarmiento, an Argentinean journalist, expressed shock that the gilded dome of the St. Charles Exchange Hotel in New Orleans had "called up my memory of St. Peters in Rome." The hotel could be seen "from all positions of the compass as if it were the only thing there…At last I was going to see in the United States a basilica designed along classic lines and on a scale dignified enough for religion."[1]

In addition to the physical grandeur commented upon was the social aspect of hotels, especially the ability of Americans to live their lives in public among those they knew only casually, if at all. This use of hotel lobbies, restaurants, and bars seemed very strange, and not particularly desirable, to European observers who were more comfortable with privacy and in restricting their social life to those they knew.

Edith Wharton and Henry James, two American arbiters of culture and mores, regarded American hotels with European eyes, scorning the social fluidity which these hotels allowed. For them, hotels represented the crass side of America, symbols of the disintegration of the old society. Edith Wharton's novelistic hotels are centers of overdecorated bad taste beloved by the nouveaux riches, sites where her characters overstep or disregard social boundaries and, as a result, descend toward humiliation and despair.[2]

For Henry James, the brash commercial display of wealth and the vast number of Americans who participated in the new hotel society were a bafflement. As early as 1870, he wrote of the maidens at a Saratoga resort that "she dresses for publicity. The thought fills you with a kind of awe. The social order of tradition is far way indeed…" Despite their being extraordinary, these hotels for James promoted a "social sameness." Forty years later, New York's Waldorf-Astoria prompted a combination of wonder and distaste at its "halls and saloons in which art and history, in masquerading dress, … stood smirking on its passage with the last cynicism of hypocrisy. The exhibition is wonderful for that, for the suggested sense of a promiscuity which manages to be at the same time an inordinate untempered monotony." Although he looked at the Waldorf-Astoria with disdain, James admitted that this gregariousness and social display conveyed "the ache of envy of the spirit of a society which had found there, in its prodigious public setting, so exactly what it wanted."

American hotel origins are usually traced to Barnum's City Hotel in Baltimore (1825–1826) and, four years later, to the Tremont House in Boston. The latter's commanding location, occupying an entire block and towering (at four stories) above its neighbors, reflected its impact on the city. A force in the city's social life, it was famous for public facilities that were available to guests and nonguests alike.

The Tremont's interior spaces were grand. A columned portico announced the street entrance, and an imposing interior stair brought one to a central rotunda leading to a choice of many public rooms. The entire first floor was given over to a full range of public functions: a 200-seat restaurant, drawing rooms, and reading rooms (the provision of separate ladies' and gentlemen's sitting rooms necessitated some duplication). The public rooms were sumptuous, finished with marble, mosaics, and fine woods. The style hearkened to the finest that the French had to offer.

The Tremont also saw the beginning of the hotel lobby, which separated the functions of the hotel from those of the restaurant and bar. No longer was the clerk of the hotel responsible for everything—rooms, food, and drinks—as in the tavern or inn. One went directly from the street into the lobby to register and to enter the other public rooms. The bartender or restaurant manager was responsible for other functions. From the start, the lobby was lavish. Although it had no specific functions that created revenue, such as the bar or restaurant, its design and psychological importance were quickly appreciated and the expenditure justified.[3]

The traditions of innovation and of flaunting the latest and largest in design and modern technical conveniences had begun. Hotel building and design quickly became a series of firsts, a constant game of one-upmanship. The Tremont House was built in reaction to the City Hotel. Just six years later, in 1836, the Astor House in New York specifically set out to dwarf its competition and to

claim for New York the reputation of having the best hotel in the Union. Its entrance soon became a prime city location in which to see and be seen.

HOTELS AS BUSINESS; HOTELS AND BUSINESS

The history of hotels is linked with money—the money to build them and the money to use them. Although understanding the social forces that gave rise to the hotel in America is important, it must also be acknowledged that at its roots the American urban hotel was a real estate transaction. In the 1800s, stock companies, created to finance construction, were an innovation introduced by American businesses. Fortified with money from investors, these companies raised the large capital required to build on a grand and lavish scale. Later on, in America and Europe, railroad companies became the entities with sufficient resources to finance these hotels.

The rapid rise in popularity of hotels derived in part from the fact that the hotel was not merely a home away from home; for many Americans in the nineteenth century, the hotel was home. Americans were often residents of urban hotels, not just travelers passing through. Many reasons have been proposed for this phenomenon ranging from the innate mobility of the American populace to the lack of servants creating difficulty in establishing permanent households. It was also the custom of a certain class to have two social seasons with two separate loci: the city in the winter and the country in the summer. To avoid maintaining two households, many spent their city time in hotels, which facilitated household and hospitality functions. Entertaining business and social colleagues was, in fact, often easier and more grand in hotel banquet rooms than at home. It should not be forgotten that, especially in the West and Midwest, single men needed the services of hotels, being more intent on seeking their fortunes than creating households. These long-term and permanent residents expanded the demand for communal public social rooms, a marked difference from what had occurred previously in America and certainly in Europe.

Although foreign commentators were impressed that anyone who could afford the price of a drink was allowed to frequent these hotels, they were equally struck with an American's ability to talk about money in public and flaunt new found riches. The barbershop in Chicago's Palmer House arcade even had silver dollars imbedded in its floor. As Rudyard Kipling commented, "They told me to go to the Palmer House which is a gilded and mirrored rabbit warren, and where I found a huge hall of tessellated marble, crammed with people talking about money." Ostentatious wealth had indeed found its stage.

HOTELS AND CITIES

Historic events of cities became intertwined with the pivotal civic, social, and business roles of hotels. Not only did New York, Chicago, Washington, and San Francisco have their famous hotels, but St. Louis, Cincinnati, and Dallas did as

(Left) The Auditorium was designed in 1889 by Dankmar Adler and Louis Sullivan as a mixed-use building combining a 400-room hotel, opera house, offices, and restaurants. The weightiness of the building is reflected in the stubby columns under large capitals and heavy beams. Sullivan's use of ornament is evident in the intricate carvings. (Chicago Architectural Photographing Company/David R. Phillips)

well. In fact, in order to be called a city, a metropolis needed a defining hotel. While the specifics of the story differ from city to city, its theme remains the same. A successful hotel becomes so connected with the pulse and imagination of its city that it crops up in its literature and mythology.

Typical of the political hotel was New York's old Fifth Avenue Hotel, which in the 1800s was the office of Tom Platt, boss of the New York State Republican party. During a perhaps less representative era than now, it was said that the future of New York and its politics were determined in the hotel's bar. The bar, at the rear of the hotel, was so situated that patrons were required to walk down a long corridor, being screened several times before entry. Depending on who you were, this procession was either one of intimidation or one of warmth and welcome. Midway through this passage were two plush red benches, dubbed the Amen Corner. No fewer than nine American presidents sat there to confer about the critical issues of the day.[4] These benches were so indicative of their time and place that they were rescued when the hotel was demolished and offered to the Museum of the City of New York.

As railroads propelled America westward, railroad companies greatly influenced real estate and hotel development either by outright ownership or by increasing the value of land along the train routes. In many cities, before the trains came through a hotel would be built to increase the importance of a town and influence the location of the line. Tower City in Cleveland, which includes shops and offices as well as a hotel, was built to entice a new railroad station.

One of the most famous hotel-railroad developments occurred around Grand Central Terminal in New York. Many hotels cropped up around the terminal, the most famous being the Biltmore. This hotel was adjacent to the terminal itself and was owned jointly by its then operators, the New York Central and the New York, New Haven, Hartford railroad companies. In fact, the hotel was built over the rails leading into the terminal, and the hotel's lobby was actually connected to the station.

Railroad schedules also influenced hotels, a fact that the Chicago's Ambassador East actively used to encourage stars to mingle with the city's elite. Designed with a ceiling that would not absorb sound, its Pump Room became the place to be seen and heard. The Pump Room with its famous Booth One was popular during the 1930s because the Chicago layover in the transcontinental railroad, the 20th Century Limited, allowed celebrities on their New York-Los Angeles voyages to stop over for entertainment and a nightcap.

QUEST FOR THE BEST: VANGUARDS AND PHOENIXES

Hotels and Fire

The history of hotels is incomplete without the mention of fire. Fire haunts hotels. Hotels routinely burn to the ground in spectacular conflagrations. Like phoenixes, they immediately reinvent themselves to be larger, more up-to-date, and of course, more fire proofed (or at least advertised as such). In fact, fire was so common that some sites burned several times. The Tremont House in Chicago was destroyed three times and rebuilt four times between 1839 and 1873.

Two major disasters that directly affected hotel development were the 1871 Chicago fire and the 1906 San Francisco earthquake with its subsequent devastating fire. In both cities, existing hotels were destroyed and in most cases, in a spirit of irrepressible civic pride and obligation, were immediately replaced.

The necessity of combating the perpetual danger of hotel fire propelled technological progress. Structural improvements such as fireproof construction were implemented and, of course, cited in advertisements as proof of the most advanced standards of security available. The Palmer House, two years after the Chicago Fire of 1871, prominently proclaimed that it was "The Only Fire-Proof Hotel in America!"

Comfort and Service

Tantalizing as it is, style isn't everything. Successful hotels unite design with technology: The hotel's image must function. We look to hotel lobbies and bars for effortlessly providing the civilizing services that make life easier. In fact, the very definition of hotel embodies the idea of a place where one's needs are attended and comfort assured. The latest inventions and gadgets are applied so that minimum effort is exerted or indeed perceived. Vanguards of the good life, hotels usher in new conveniences and services from the introduction of indoor plumbing and central heating in the 1800s to the modern fitness and business centers of today. In fact, no hotel has been known to provide any service not billed as "state of the art."

Elegant luxury, far from being solely visual, requires that one's needs are satisfied, unobtrusively and with grace. Technology is pressed into service to furnish the greatest number of conveniences at the most modern level achievable. To fulfill this ambition, mechanical services and systems purport to be always one step ahead of the present—models of efficiency, safety, and comfort. As is so often the fate of those ahead of their times, the history of hotel building abounds with innovation and obsolescence, a constant cycle of never-befores and past-their-primes.

In America, hotels were the proving grounds for quality of life innovations and the rise of technology in the service of comfort. And in hotels, lobbies and public rooms first flaunted the newest conveniences and inventions. In the 1800s, hotel design routinely incorporated plumbing, heating, electrical, and other advances before they became widely available. In fact, either from necessity, competition, or whim, hotels showcased (and continue to do so today) the latest improvements and hitherto unavailable services.

Once advances were introduced, their widespread use and refinement were rapid and inevitable. For example, in 1829, Boston's Tremont House boasted of eight water closets on the ground floor and gaslight in its vast public rooms. (The hotel had its own water system before the Boston waterworks were installed.) Just six years later, the Astor House in New York proudly claimed to be the first hotel to have plumbing facilities on every floor as well as gaslighting throughout.

The Palmer House's Tiffany's angel still stands at the entrance of its Empire Room. [Palmer House (Tony Romano)]

Thereafter, hotel building in the nineteenth century presents itself as a series of firsts: the first public rooms heated by steam (Eastern Exchange Hotel, Boston, 1846); the first to enjoy passenger elevator service (Fifth Avenue Hotel, New York, 1859); the first public rooms to be lit by electricity (Hotel Everett, New York, and the Palmer House, Chicago, 1882); the first subscribers to new telephone exchanges (1879).

Hotel design during the nineteenth century heralded this new technology as a source for celebration and wonder. The means of producing the comforts of life were out in the open, advertised for all to see. The light fixtures presiding over the grand lobby of Chicago's Palmer House, for instance, could be seen as a mythical image of a goddess bringing light to humanity (figure done by Tiffany).

Toward the end of the nineteenth century, as technology proceeded apace, expression in design became subdued and often hidden. Incorporating technological advancement in design has meant masking the new within the forms of the old, with designs that recall the past, not proclaim the future. As unobtrusive as the silent service of the waiter who anticipates diners' every needs, mechanical conveniences are absorbed in the overall design, invisible servants disguised within motifs of former eras and far-off places.

Frank expression of technology, a theoretical underpinning of modern aesthetic movements, is almost nonexistent in hotel lobby design. After the enthusiastic nineteenth century embrace of mechanical advances, exhilaration in expressing details of the comfortable life is seldom seen.

Appearing fifty or even several hundred years behind the times while functioning years ahead is the hotel design maxim. Hotels of both old-world elegance and nonwestern design (in America or elsewhere) have obliterated visual references to the twentieth century while enjoying its physical comforts. The means of the twentieth century's ability to heat, light, and communicate are often undetectable when one walks through replicas of French chateaux or English country houses.

Technological invisibility does not in any way imply dispensability. Obsolescent facilities are often the cause of a hotel's demise, a failure of not keeping pace with an expected level of convenience, rather than design. The fabled Chicago Auditorium Hotel designed by Adler and Sullivan, for example, was seen as outmoded and inefficient because not all the rooms had bathroom facilities. This, in America, is an untenable situation.

In hotels, prosaic services are raised to an elegant, if rarefied, level, accented and exaggerated above their merely functional requirements. It is the restrooms where function, luxury, and inventiveness coalesce. Indeed, the acid test of a hotel lobby's design is the men's and women's rooms. How creatively the familiar is manipulated, how flattering the lighting and mirrors, and how elegant the materials are the measurements of the design theme's success.

Elegance is conveyed not only through the use of expensive materials but from the generous, indeed profligate, use of space. Good restrooms do not cramp the stalls or treat people as if they were in the average bus terminal. Water closets, and sometimes even sinks, are ensconced in their own rooms, with partitions to the ceiling ensuring privacy. These rooms become true oases, places to refresh and regroup.

The design theme is usually continued in the restrooms: French provincial design requires white and gold trimmed stalls; modern, the expressive use of good materials without applied decoration; cutting-edge, a witty look at the mundane, almost a reinvention of the wheel.

Chapter 4

BARS AND SPECIAL ROOMS

The prototype of the living-room lobby, the Algonquin's comfortable armchairs and sofas are scattered around in informal groupings. When almost all furniture and finishes were replaced to replicate the original during a recent renovation, its ambiance of shabby chic vanished. History still seeps into the atmosphere and makes this bar one of the more sophisticated meeting spots in midtown New York. (Algonquin Hotel)

THE SPIRIT of a hotel is best defined by its bar. The lobby sets the stage as the place that impresses; the bar brings that feeling home. Hotel bars, along with tearooms, palm courts, and rooftop lounges, are designed solely for our entertainment, amusement, and comfort. For the price of a glass of Beaujolais or a hot pot of Earl Grey, we can savor the experience of luxury, the club, or international high style, even if we can't afford the price of the rooms above. The office during a business trip, the home base in a foreign country, the rendezvous after work: Bars and special rooms are worldwide meeting places.

From the beginning, hotel bars strove to raise themselves above the lowly saloon. Seeking ever more exotic ways to differentiate themselves from the commonplace, novelty, and attentive service became their keynotes which remain today. Emphasizing the hotel connection, hotel bars maintain a formal tone and purpose, stressing the difference between the everyday and a special occasion. They are destinations where demeanor and dress are expected to match the decor.

The cocktail, which some rank as one of America's greatest contributions to the civilized world, parallels the story of hotel bars. The hotel's search for distinctiveness and innovation directly led to the cult of the cocktail. Masters of concoction, of both the classic and spectacularly absurd variety, hotel bartenders create, not just serve, special cocktails. Mixed drinks and the places in which to enjoy them came to be seen as a defining national trait. The universal sign, AMERICAN BAR, survives this golden era of invention. A somewhat wry

The Waldorf-Astoria's Bull and Bear Bar: Dark wood, polished brass railings, and tufted leather constitute the main ingredients of this clubby, business bar. The namesake bronze statue has stolidly stood by during the ups and downs that have defined New York's financial markets since its installation in 1897. This latest design recalls the original four-sided standing bar. After Prohibition, New York State law mandated seats at a bar, prohibiting standing bars. (Lou Hammond & Assoc, Inc.)

political statement in Europe during Prohibition, those neon block English letters still dot windows of the world, understood no matter what the native language.

When not part of the lobby, hotel bars are laboratories for new design ideas. Taking advantage of contained space and frequent renovations, design experimentation is common. By having several bars or lounges, hotels are free to create special atmospheres for different occasions and tastes. In contrast, because of its larger size and need for consistent identity, a lobby's design tends to remain constant in image if not in detail.

Bar style parallels the designs and whims of the times. Exotic venues inspired by international expositions flourished at the turn of the century. The last vestiges of Art Deco influenced repeal design. Moldings, details, and history were stripped from walls in the sixties, only to be returned in the eighties. Throughout, however, bar design has proclaimed one constant—the vaunting of the unusual or the excessive. When thematic uniqueness is not desired, the goal then turns into the search for the ultimate in acknowledged elegance or tradition.

SOCIAL STUDIES

Writers, entertainers, politicians, and stockbrokers have all claimed hotel bars as special enclaves, their places to congregate, socialize, and conduct business. The bar can define a hotel and establish its reputation. Catering to special groups, making them comfortable, and meeting their needs have always been hallmarks of a good urban hotel. Thus it is not uncommon for hotels to become famous for their bar habitués rather than for their services, design, or quality of the rooms.

It would be impossible to comment on this phenomenon without citing one of its most well-known instances. Over fifty years ago, the Round Table wits parried aphorisms at the Algonquin Hotel in New York. It is the rare person today who fails to mention this upon walking into the hotel. The Algonquin's lobby is its bar. The epitome of an English clubroom, comfortable couches and armchairs are clustered around coffee tables creating small groupings scattered about the room. Another smaller bar hidden behind this large room is for those who desire more privacy.

Across the street, the Royalton has recently been reincarnated as a hotel catering to writers of the nineties. Although the stylistic opposite of the Algonquin, it functions almost identically. Its lobby is its bar, which has quickly become the place to be in midtown New York. The hotel provides books, magazines, and even game boards to encourage people to actively use the room. The Royalton also has other bars and meeting places for those who want to avoid the openness.

Almost every group has called at least one hotel its own. In New York, businessmen claimed the Bull and Bear Bar in the old Waldorf Hotel on 34th Street, where, at its four-sided standing bar, robber barons drank and businessmen from out of town converged. Today, the bar is totally separated from the lobby, having, instead, a strong street presence and entrance. In fact, it's possible to patronize the bar and not realize that you are in a hotel. It presents a solid, hefty scale and massiveness, as if to assert its unabashed pride in being a bar.

Business of another style is conducted across the country behind the lush green excess of the Beverly Hills Hotel's gardens. The overgrown landscape surrounds the pink Mission Revival palace whose interior carpets, wallpaper, and details reprise the jungle paradise outside. A recent extensive renovation by Gensler Associates, Los Angeles, and Hirsch Bedner & Associates re-created the hotel's fabled past. Renowned for its famous clientele, its lobby, and restaurant, the Polo Lounge, have entered the lexicon of Hollywood deals and affairs.

In 1949, Paul Revere Williams added a sleek new wing to the original 1912 building. An architect to the stars and a master of curvilinear Art Deco, Williams created the public rooms for exhibiting the artifice for which Los Angeles is known and made the niches and private spaces within these rooms conducive to serious business.

Prohibition

Any discussion of American hotel bars must acknowledge the impact of Prohibition, which lasted over thirteen years, from January 16, 1920, through December 5, 1933. Although Prohibition caused the demise of many establishments, paradoxically, it prevailed during a hotel building boom (in 1933, about 50 percent of hotels never had any bar facilities). Repeal demanded that the integration of bars, cocktail lounges, and similar facilities into hotel social life be considered anew.

Reverting to pre-Prohibition designs was not possible. During the early 1900s, main floors of hotels still provided separate men's and women's reception rooms

(Overleaf) The Royalton recasts the role of the living-room lobby in a cutting-edge mode. The blue carpet is the spine and organizing feature of the room. Raised several steps above most of the seating, this is a wonderful vantage point to see who is there before plunging in to become part of the action. This is the hotel bar in its purest theatrical form. Aside from the blue carpet, the palette is muted and neutral, allowing people to provide the color. (Tom Vack/The Royalton)

(Above) Beverly Hills Hotel: Adjacent to the lobby and only slightly more restrained is the new, intimate Tea Lounge. Here, visual interest is found in the furnishings and surface treatments, not the architectural space or details. Although the railing and the artwork repeat the organic theme, windows bring glimpses of the real garden into the room. The gold-leaf piano introduces artifice into nature. The soft pastel palette unifies this room with the rest of the hotel.
(Beverly Hills Hotel/Fred Licht)

(Below) Beverly Hills Hotel: The circular green booths and pink tablecloths of the Polo Lounge are more famous for their diners than for their design. The soft, curvilinear plan and details as well as the color scheme of the original design have been maintained through the renovation. (Beverly Hills Hotel/Fred Licht)

(Left) The exuberant spirit of nature from outside bursts into the lobby of the Beverly Hills Hotel, originally designed by Paul Williams. The signature banana-leaf motif, seen here in the carpet and plants, repeats throughout the hotel. The lobby is all curves and excess in pink, green, and peach as one space gently slides into another. The rounded furniture, heavy columns, ceiling patterns, moldings, and light fixtures all serve to make this a glamorous living room stage set.
(Beverly Hills Hotel/Fred Licht)

(Above) The Hotel Bel Air's wood-paneled, cozy living-room bar completes the fantasy journey up a long, winding canyon road. A favored rendezvous spot for Los Angeles elite, the room's decor embodies the encyclopedia of traditional, country estate design from its gilt-framed dog painting, to the soft, upholstered furniture, to the obligatory fireplace. The northerness of the bar contrasts with the hotel's exterior: a red-tiled, lushly landscaped, pink and gray stuccoed California paradise.

(Bel-Air Hotel)

The Gallery Bar at the Biltmore is the watering spot in downtown Los Angeles. The detailing of this room is highly ornate; the colors and furniture contrast with warmth and simplicity. Although the room is narrow, the high ceiling creates a pleasing, comfortable volume. Adjacent to this room is the Cognac Room, a more intimate space.

(The Biltmore, Los Angeles)

(Above) William Powell and Myrna Loy, as the sophisticated urban couple Nick and Nora Charles in The Thin Man, chose hotel bars as the preferred place to catch up on their martinis. (© Turner Entertainment Co. All Rights Reserved.)

(Right) The Redwood Room at the Clift Hotel: San Francisco's glorious celebration of the end of Prohibition remains an Art Deco masterpiece. A mural created of inlaid heartwood rests above the bar, which was constructed from redwood burl and Italian marble. At its edge, brass elephant heads raise their trunks to circle upon brass railings (a design conceit recalling the days when provision of "crying towels" at the edges of bars was commonplace). The massive, round proportions embraced by that era are repeated here in the round marble table tops and red plush barrel chairs. (Clift Hotel)

and cafes. According to proponents of the Volstead Act, drinking establishments were often male enclaves—gloomy, smoky centers of drunkenness. Repeal entailed the presumption that women would comprise a vital part of the new clientele, demanding designs that stressed cleanliness and comfort. These hotel bars and cocktail lounges were expected to be open, well-lit, and accessible. Indeed, the repeal design goal was to make bars respectable.

Putting a public, social face on drinking assumed priority. Fearing a return to dark, dirty male bastions, and perhaps government reprisals, hotel bars strove to be rooms that women would enjoy. Thus the cocktail lounge was born, a place for polite conversation, sparkling wit, and dancing, not messy besottedness.

Nick and Nora Charles of *The Thin Man* fame gave form to this desired image, drinking endless martinis in movieland's Normandie Hotel. Engaging in clever repartee while solving mysteries, they embodied the sophisticated urban couple, with hotels their venues of choice. As testament to the acceptability of drinking, the bar scenes are among the most brightly lit in the film, filled with sounds of sparkling conversation and clinking glasses.

Repeal occurred during the depths of the Depression and the last years of Art Deco influence. Art Deco's allusions to luxury and sumptuousness teamed up with the redefinition of the bar as modern and sophisticated. It was a perfect marriage. Imparting class to bars and drinking establishments, Art Deco was the design source of some of the most dramatic, insular stages created to forget the economic ills outside. A few of the best are still around today.

The Redwood Room in the Clift Hotel, San Francisco's most glorious celebration of the end of Prohibition, remains an Art Deco masterpiece. Designed in 1934 by G. Albert Lansburgh, who was also responsible for the interior of San Francisco's Opera House, its sense of theatricality shines through. All surfaces of the lounge—walls, columns, ceiling—are sheathed in aged and polished "curly" redwood, enveloping the room in a deep, rich glow. A contrast of dark and light, its Art Deco-inspired light sconces dot the room while the golds of Gustav Klimt reproductions glimmer on the dark walls.

Timothy Pflueger, an influential San Francisco architect, designed some classic post-Prohibition rooms in his hometown. The first was the Fairmont Hotel's Le Cirque Lounge, built in 1934 and recently restored. Mirrors installed on varying planes reflect curved forms. Etched glass and shiny ceilings activate the room, even when unoccupied. The perimeter wall murals by Bruton have gold-leaf backgrounds, their swirling, energetic forms creating yet more movement and glitter. The room shimmers. The crowning touch is a pyramid of newly legal liquor bottles, proudly displayed as trophies of a hard-fought battle.

Five years later, the same designer removed most of the solid exterior walls of the highest floor of the Mark Hopkins Hotel and created new vistas for hotel bar design. Pflueger's discreet design of the Top of the Mark allows the eye to skim the room to the view outside. Nothing obscures the scene beyond its windows. All elements, including the bar, are lower than eye level and do not interfere with the panorama. Not even the prized bottles, which were otherwise center stage, interrupt the seemingly infinite line of vision.

ART AND DRINK

Murals and hotel bars are made for each other. Although drinking is not normally associated with art, the prevalence of murals and other artforms in bars cannot be ignored. Used perhaps only to name the bar or to encourage conversation among strangers, murals furnish a design focus while bestowing individuality and enshrining the bar's uniqueness.

Art styles have gone through many phases. During the barroom's male enclave period, paintings of nudes and nondescript landscapes were the norm. In New York during the early 1900s, down the street from Republican deal making, Democrats at the Hoffman House struck their bargains under the watchful eye of Bouguereau's 12- by 8-ft *Nymph and Satyr,* one of the most famous barroom nudes in America, more for its overwhelming size and subject than for its artistry. The old Waldorf bar boasted a bucolic scene portrayed in an oil painting entitled *Sheep Seeking Shelter from the Storm.* Patrons no longer capable of pronouncing the title were asked to leave.

Around the turn of the century, when not portraying nudes or nondescript landscapes, bar art also depicted uplifting images of ancient myths or the enshrinement of such noble principles as Truth or Beauty. The move to more decorative and entertaining art was probably made for economic reasons. A contemporary critic in *The Architectural Record* attributed the change to Maxfield Parrish's mural, *Old King Cole,* in the former Knickerbocker Hotel bar in New York. The hotel was built in 1906 specifically to attract the crowd in the emerging theater district. Its owner, Colonel John Jacob Astor, commissioned a mural to be amusing, decorative, and architecturally significant. The bar became one of the most popular of its day, a feat credited to the novelty of the lighthearted theme of the mural. As with all good and successful ideas, it was imitated.

The popularity of *King Cole* brought Parrish two other hotel bar mural commissions based on fairy tale-nursery rhyme themes. *Sing a Song of Sixpence,* in Chicago's Hotel Sherman, was destroyed along with the hotel. In 1909, three years after the disastrous fire, Parrish painted *The Pied Piper* for San Francisco's Palace Hotel reopening. This bar still maintains its popularity with the surrounding business community.

Not all art is painted. Architectural terra cotta has been used to great effect to create interesting, grottolike rooms that found favor at the beginning of this century. From its inauguration in 1907, the Rathskeller at the Seelbach Hotel in Louisville, Kentucky, has weathered the tumultuous history of its hotel. Located in the basement, its surfaces are completely covered with the colorful and molded glazed tiles of the Cincinnati-based Rookwood Pottery Company. It is the only such room still intact (although most of the former Della Robbia Bar in New York also exists). Although it began as a bar, because of Prohibition and several hotel closings, the Rathskeller has been transformed over the years and is now mainly used as a function room.

In 1910, three years after the Rathskeller was built, Rookwood Pottery installed its largest hotel architectural terra cotta interior at New York's

(Left) Denver responded to repeal by opening the Cruise Bar at the Oxford Hotel promptly on December 5, 1933. Inspired by the lounges of the Queen Mary (hence the bar's name), this long, narrow room is a study in simplicity, of the use of lighting to an extraordinary end. Red light washes over wall decorations carved from homosote. The black lacquer finish of the bar dramatically contrasts with the room, each setting the other off to best advantage. This room is listed in the National Register of Historic Places. (Larry Laszlo/Comedia)

(Above) The Fairmont Hotel's Cirque Lounge as it looked in 1934. (Ansel Adams courtesy of John M. Pflueger Architect, AIA)

Details of the Fairmont Hotel's Cirque Lounge mural today. The room is now used for special events. (© 1986 Chuck Fishman/Fairmont Hotel)

(Left) The original Top of the Mark is serene; all its details are subtle. Just as patrons are suspended above San Francisco, the top of the circular bar floats above its base, supported at intervals by short metal posts. Softness and roundness are reiterated in the tufted front of the bar's base, lollipop bar stools, and comfortable chairs. Pflueger also designed the Starlight Room in the Fairmont Hotel and the Patent Leather Bar at the Westin St. Francis. (Gabriel Moulin courtesy of John M. Pflueger Architect AIA)

(Right) Rockwell Architecture's recent renovation of the Monkey Bar in the Hotel Elysée recalls the heyday of the 1930s hotel bar when Hollywood stars, writers, and personalities mingled and partied. This was not a quiet place. Tallulah Bankhead, Tennessee Williams, Marlon Brando, and others appreciated its dramatic qualities and readily transformed the bar into a real-life stage. When it opened in 1936, the walls were mirrored, which, given the clientele, only encouraged the crowd to play in front of them. Charles Vella murals replaced the mirrors, freezing and parodying the antics of the preening and pantomiming patrons in the form of monkeys. The renovation recaptures the spirit of the original in tone, color, and sense of whimsy. The murals and the monkey sconces have been restored, along with the meandering mahogany bar. Primary colors enliven the space—the gold and yellow of the murals play against the red lollipop stools and blue floor. This is a room to have fun in, luxurious and comfortable at the same time. (The Rockwell Group; Paul Warchol ©)

(Above) The Knickerbocker Hotel, in the heart of New York's theater district, was itself devoted to amusement and entertainment. Once so popular and central to the life of the New York theater world, it was called the 42nd Street Country Club. Who said that theater only took place on the stage? To this end, Maxfield Parrish's mural, Old King Cole and His Fiddlers Three, held court from its opening in 1906 until the hotel closed, unable to survive Prohibition. Folklore attributes the king's fiddler's and jesters' joviality to the supposed flatulence of the king. While acknowledging this as a possible interpretation, Parrish denied that it was his intent. To modern eyes, the Knickerbocker's room appears bare, its surfaces hard, and furnishings minimal. Judging from contemporaneous reports, the room relied upon the force of personalities of its patrons as well as from its art. Note the stand-up bar, which was the norm during pre-Prohibition times. (MCNY/The Byron Collection)

(Right) After a brief stay at the Racquet Club, the King Cole mural was transferred to the St. Regis Hotel in 1935, where it remains today. At the end of the lobby corridor and around the Astor Court (itself presenting murals of a decidedly earlier tradition), Old King Cole provides light, color, and focus as sure as he did at the Knickerbocker. This room is softer and more plush than the original. The colors of the dark-paneled lounge, as seen in the carpet and upholstery, mutely reflect the mural. The change of clientele from actors and promoters to international businesspeople has subdued the atmosphere somewhat. (Eleanor Lambert Ltd. for The St. Regis Hotel)

(Above) At the Pied Piper Bar in San Francisco's Sheraton Palace Hotel, as at the St. Regis, Parrish's mural is the focus of the room. Polished wood and muted colors complement the colors of the mural. Recent renovation uncovered a marble mosaic floor buried underneath old carpeting. Emphasis was given to restoring the bar's original features such as polishing the oak paneling, maintaining elaborate chandeliers, and brightening the lighting from the glass ceiling. The painting on the wood beams is new.
(Sheraton Palace Hotel)

The Rotunda at New York's Pierre Hotel envelops the room in a three-dimensional fantasy. Note the suspended cloud obscuring the heating diffuser. (Pierre Hotel)

(Above) The Della Robbia Bar at the
Vanderbilt Hotel: The room still survives, not
as a hotel nor as a bar, but as the Fiori
Restaurant. It was recently designated a New
York City landmark.
(Cincinnnati Historical Society)

(Left) The Rathskeller at the Seelbach
Hotel: The stubby columns take their job of
holding up the whole building very seriously.
The groin vaults simultaneously give the
room a great sense of height and volume
while creating a grottolike atmosphere.
(Seelbach Hotel)

Vanderbilt Hotel, about ten blocks south of Grand Central Terminal. Occupying the ground floor of the hotel, the Della Robbia Bar and Grill, named after the Florentine family of ceramic artists, was soon nicknamed "The Crypt" because of its low-profile vaulted ceiling. Designed by Warren & Wetmore, the bar featured thin-shell Guastavino vaults, which were a popular construction method in the early part of the century. The herringbone pattern of the vaults, bordered by the colorful and molded bands of tile at the arches, creates the decoration of the bar.

PALM COURTS

The center of the traditional lobby is often the palm court, the civilizing heart of the hotel. Today, its only requirement is to be named such; palms and plants are optional. Usually skylit or, if not possible, artificially lit to simulate a sky above, it is the genteel place for social events such as afternoon tea.

The palm court descended from the exterior courtyard, which provided vehicular access to the building and the required daylight to guest rooms above. As hotels became bigger, often occupying whole city blocks, efficient floor layouts to allow light and air into the guest rooms frequently used courtyards in some version of the U or W shape. Building a glass roof over the area open to the sky at the main floor transformed that space into a bright, sun-filled room. By keeping plants and forsaking vehicles, hotels created a warm, inviting atmosphere.

The most impressive existing skylit room today is located in San Francisco's Sheraton Palace, which replaced the original hotel destroyed in the fire following the 1906 earthquake. Trowbridge and Livingston (also architects of the St. Regis Hotel) reinterpreted the hotel's trademark court. Deciding not to re-create an atrium, with the rooms overlooking it, the designers capped the 8000 ft^2 court with stained glass and dubbed it the Garden Court, the physical and emotional center of the hotel. Recently renovated, the room again sparkles, its surfaces gilded and bathed with daylight through its newly cleaned glass.

The Garden Court is not an intimate space, but one that, through its massive scale, rich materials, and elaborate fittings, conveys its public importance. Although large, the skylight's profusion of detail, such as its small-scale glass ribbing, grid and patterned glass, as well as the details on the Ionic columns and entablature that support the dome's large span, all serve to personalize the room, breaking down the scale for human use.

In more public times, the Garden Court acted as San Francisco's living room. Despite its size and volume, historic photos show comfortable, almost intimate, furniture arrangements. From small gatherings, to chance encounters, to solitary newspaper reading, the ease of social interaction and daily urban life is easily imaginable. (Chicago's Palmer House lobby, of similar scale and pomp, probably was used in the same manner.) Today, by contrast, the room needs four times the amount of furniture to fill it up.

By 1900, the palm court was *de rigueur* at all hotels of a certain class. Often adjacent to the restaurant and cafe, it might have been the only public room where both sexes could meet and smoke. At that time, New York welcomed two very different, but equally influential, interpretations of the palm court: the Ritz Carlton (1910) and the Astor Hotel (1904). The former was sedate, a model of quiet elegance; the latter was all whimsy and ostentation.

Warren & Wetmore, architects remembered today mostly for Grand Central Terminal, achieved their reputation through their hotels, such as the 1912 Biltmore and the 1910 Ritz Carlton. The Ritz Carlton, whose design reflected a resurgence in the popularity of the English neoclassical architect Robert Adam, quickly inaugurated a new style dubbed Ritz Hotel Adam. Located between the hotel's lobby and its oval restaurant, its palm court is an intimate two-story room. A slight barrel vault ceiling, rounded balconies jutting into the room with mirror-paned doors, and overflowing plants lend the room interest, detail, and a garden informality. In contrast, the Astor Hotel's L'Orangerie was a cross-roads of social activity, a place where both the patrons and the rooms showed off. Scenographic methods transformed the barrel vault and room into different settings.

Today, bars and tearooms are often the center of hotels' social activity, over-shadowing lobbies in importance. During creative renovations of historic hotels, the saving of special rooms and their reemergence as bars or tearooms recapture the feeling of the hotel bar as an urban destination.

One of the more notable examples of this phenomenon is the New York Palace Hotel. During the late 1970s and after a contentious fight, the McKim, Mead & White-designed Villard Houses on Madison Avenue across from Saint Patrick's Cathedral were incorporated into a new hotel that rose up behind it. The town-houses' U-shaped courtyard was turned into a grand entrance, and several previously private rooms were transformed into the hotel's main public spaces. The Gold Room, originally designed as a music room, is a particularly wonderful result of this compromise.

Philadelphia witnessed the survival and transformation of the Bellevue-Stratford into the Hotel Atop the Bellevue. Built at the same time as the Willard Hotel in Washington, to even more favorable reviews, the Bellevue-Stratford was famous for its spectacular oval staircases rising throughout the structure, lighting fixtures by Thomas Edison, and large corner rooftop cupolas. It was high society's hotel before its crippling, painfully slow demise that culminated in its being the site of the VFW convention that named Legionnaire's Disease.

Its renovation entailed its dissection into a mixed-use building consisting of the hotel, offices, and ground floor stores and restaurants. Although essentially an urban mall, the street lobby, which retains the scale and detail of the old hotel, functions for all the new occupants. The main hotel bar and tearooms are on top of the building, accessible by elevators.

The magic and importance of these special rooms, with palms or without, endure today. More genteel than a bar (although certainly alcohol is served), more informal than a restaurant, yet more commercial than an open lobby, special rooms carve out their niches to become standard-bearers of urbaneness and distinctive design.

(Above) The Garden Court at the Sheraton Palace Hotel was originally used as San Francisco's living room. Furniture is scattered around in varying configurations suitable for small group conversations or for individual activities such as reading or writing. Individual rugs over the marble floor further break up the scale of the room and recall a residential setting. (Sheraton Palace Hotel)

(Right) Today, the Garden Court is a restaurant, serving all meals including the all important afternoon tea. (Sheraton Palace Hotel)

(Far left top) The genteel good taste of a bygone era shines through in this photo of the old Ritz Carlton, which established a new standard of the intimate, exclusive urban hotel. Although filled with tables, chairs, palms, and flowers, the architecture of the room itself is quite simple and direct. (MCNY/The Byron Collection)

(Far left bottom) Parading and posing are evident in this contemporaneous sketch of the Astor Hotel's social scene. The room, known as L'Orangerie, was transformed into a vision of the Mediterranean through lighting and scenographic effects. Hanging plants, oversized urns, and arched podiums completed the picture. (MCNY/ The Byron Collection)

(Left) The arched entrance to the lobby lounge at the Mayfair Hotel in New York. (Mayfair Hotel)

(Below) The Mayfair Hotel's lobby lounge is a quiet room adaptable for breakfast, lunch, or tea, as comfortable for business as for pleasure. The carved ceiling, columned arches, and raised esplanade around the sunken court all supply detail, interest, and variety. (Mayfair Hotel)

(Above) Seattle's Sorrento Hotel Fireside
Lounge's tiled fireplace and polished
mahogany replicate residential coziness.
(Sorrento Hotel)

(Left) The Heathman Hotel, Portland,
Oregon: Often the comfort of the living room
is preferred to the formality of the palm
court. Large space and tables are exchanged
for fireplaces and informal furniture
groupings. The Heathman Hotel has served
downtown Portland since its opening in
1927. Its two-story-high lobby lounge with
its wood paneling, inviting fireplace, and
warm colors is the setting for afternoon tea
as well as musical evenings. (Heathman Hotel)

(Left) Having tea within the cupola at the Hotel Atop the Bellevue is a bit like being on the inside of a robin's egg. The high domed space with its large arched windows overlooks Philadelphia. The painting around the oculus lends the room the needed scale. (Simon Public Relations Group, Inc.)

(Below) Philadelphia's Hotel Atop the Bellevue's public rooms, except the entrance lobby, were relocated to upper floors. The Library Bar is worth the elevator ride to it. The dark wood paneling, intimate lighting, and warm red furnishings and carpets create an out-of-the-way, private retreat. The library theme recalls that, at the turn of the century, hotels traditionally had lending libraries often before their cities did. This room, complete with the day's newspaper, could just as easily be located in an English country estate. (Simon Public Relations Group, Inc.)

(Left) The Gold Room at the New York Palace Hotel: Originally the music room in the Villard Houses, its decoration is traced to Stanford White (of McKim, Mead & White fame) who applied triple gold leaf to the ceiling and transformed the room into his vision of an Italian Renaissance palazzo. The paintings at both ends of the room are by John La Farge and represent Music and Drama. Stained-glass windows, which originally faced a courtyard but now are blocked by the new building, are artificially lit and backed with aluminum and Plexiglas, mimicking an imaginary light source. A harpist entertains during teatime. (The Zimmerman Agency)

Chapter 5

THE GLORIOUS PAST: OLD-WORLD ELEGANCE IN AMERICA

Dedicated to yesterday's charm and tomorrow's convenience.
Engraving on new york's hampshire house

DEEP INSIDE the recesses of the American unconscious lies the enduring conviction that traditional European forms and materials define elegance. This was true in the mid-1800s, and it is still true today. Old-world luxury never goes out of fashion. Although constantly reinterpreted, it sets the standard of comfort, class, and service to which all hotel design refers. The Europe that these American hotels strive to reflect is neither the peasant shelter nor the average middle-class abode, but the palaces and playgrounds of royalty.

These hotels evoke the epitome of elegance and refinement, reminiscent of other times and places. Their measure of success is how well they conjure up foreign locales while asserting their distinctive aura. Exuding opulence, they are American interpretations of European splendor. What is emulated is not an aloof or cool elegance but one of warmth and hospitality. Large volumes speak of grandeur; marble and polished wood lavish surfaces; dark, rich colors suffuse rooms with warm reds and golds.

Their design palette makes full use of the rich range of art history. Marching from medieval times through the Romanesque, Renaissance, and on to the French Second Empire, hotel designers manipulate many images, at times simultaneously, to convey splendor. Broad interpretations of all styles are (and were) quite conscious and acknowledged. Not confined to ideas and forms, borrowing extends to objects and materials. Advertisements proclaim elaborate Italian marble floors, the finest French furnishings, and paintings and sculpture gathered from European antique houses and collectors.

During the nineteenth century, just as a well-rounded American education included the "grand tour," hotel builders and architects journeyed around the

The Fairmont, San Francisco
(Fairmont Hotel)

country and Europe evaluating the latest and best developments in hotel design. The Westin St. Francis in San Francisco typified this common turn-of-the-century hotel construction process. The locally prominent Crocker family wanted the world to declare San Francisco the Paris of the West. What better way to accomplish this than to build a hotel rivaling those of the East and Europe? Situated prominently on Union Square, the proposed hotel was perfectly positioned to command the center of social and political life of the new city. Four years before opening in 1904, the architects Bliss and Faville were sent by the owners on a six-month fact-finding tour of Europe and America to determine the best the world offered and to adopt it for the design of the new hotel.

During that era, aesthetic inspiration derived from the grand hotels of London, Paris, and Vienna; technical innovations came from the emerging hotels of the East, especially the new high-rise buildings of New York, such as H. J. Hardenbergh's Waldorf-Astoria. They evidently learned their lessons well because the St. Francis lobby quickly became San Francisco's meeting place of choice, its parlors, library, and grill the preferred venues of the local elite and visiting dignitaries.

Just what hallmarks of old-world elegance did these architects use that appealed to the Victorian taste and continues to do so today? Primarily, its lobby exults in its substance and permanence. The lobby's high, decorative ceilings generate a grand sense of arrival. Two-story columns reinforce a room height usually reserved for public buildings, be it Athens or Washington. The bar, raised several steps to create a sense of entrance, distances itself from the hubbub of the lobby below. This also has the effect of lowering the bar's ceiling, giving the room a more intimate feeling.

Separation between outside and inside is clear. There is no doubt that, upon entering, one walks into a different world from that experienced on the outside. Although large and full of activity, the lobby is a haven from the noise and street life on Union Square. Its street level plan generously allows much room for meeting and congregating. The lobby is a large foyer, dispersing people to various functions—the bar, stores, telephones—before hotel functions are encountered.

Hotel lobby style stems from surfaces and furnishings as well as form. Style and colors fluctuate greatly over time within the structure and volume of the rooms. Throughout a hotel's life, the surface decoration and furnishings must change to keep pace with the stylistic sensibility of its times. Timeless fashion is anything but. The style strives for old-world elegance, not old-fashionedness. A fine line separates the two.

Change, when cleverly done, can so coincide with accepted concepts of luxury that a hotel's clientele will presume that its favorite haunt has endured the years seamlessly, with nary a digression. The metamorphoses of the lobby at the Westin St. Francis are illustrative. When it first opened, Victorian taste demanded decoration and clutter, while avoiding ostentation. In the thirties, during the Depression, style became more austere and masculine, with leathers and oriental carpets creating a worn comfort. In a modernization frenzy, postwar enthusiasm and optimism stripped away excess surface decoration and "cooled down" the room with hard surfaces and light colors. Postmodernists of the eighties re-created decoration in the quest for soft finishes and surfaces. Throughout, the marble columns and coffered ceilings inlaid with rosettes remained untouched, silent witnesses to the changing styles around them.

The Westin St. Francis has represented old-world elegance on a grand scale, located in the heart of a city, open to all. The main floor is designed for the flow of large numbers of people, its entrance wide and passageways ample. About the same time in New York City, Colonel John Jacob Astor, the builder of the St. Regis, opted for a new approach. Rather than locating at the center of business or entertainment as the competition was wont to do, his Hotel St. Regis claimed new territory—the fringes of a select residential neighborhood. Self-consciously, the architects Trowbridge and Livingston[1] designed the St. Regis as an enclave of exclusiveness dressed up in Beaux-Arts detailing.

Its grandness derived not from large spaces, but from design quality, fine materials and quality construction, and above all, its clientele. Quite unabashedly, and with the lack of humility the rest of the country expects from a New Yorker, Arthur C. David, an architecture critic writing in *The Architectural Record* in 1904, started his review by simply stating that the Hotel St. Regis "establishes a new and higher standard for the construction and decoration of hotels in a city that in this department of building establishes the standard for the whole country."[2] The article was entitled, "The St. Regis—The Best Type of Metropolitan Hotel."

Nearly a century later, the St. Regis still holds itself up to that standard. Recently unshrouded from a major renovation, it has once again chosen refined opulence over moderation, its patrons over the general public. The lobby itself is not a destination but a means to the public and private rooms beyond.

The plan of the building and lobby is long and narrow, with its length and entrances along the side street. The main entrance, perpendicular to the lobby's axis, leads directly to the hotel's main desk. The bar and eating areas are at the opposite end of the lobby, creating a slightly awkward forced promenade. The entrance and main public areas are located on the side street for economic and spiritual reasons. Present-day real estate values mandated that the Fifth Avenue facade be utilized for high-end retail stores. In addition, now as well as at the turn of the century, the hotel's bar entrance must be over 200 ft from the Fifth Avenue Presbyterian Church, located across the street. (Several blocks north, St. Patrick's Cathedral posed this problem for the Gold Room at the Palace Hotel.)

The red-carpeted entry with its original highly polished brass revolving door clearly represents the hotel's intent. Its uplifted canopy welcomes and the rich materials shine, but the entrance is small and confined. This entrance is not for crowds, flowing in and out, but for well-pampered patrons. The lobby discourages lobby loungers; however, there are small way stations (perhaps for patient escorts and spouses) along the promenade to the tea court and King Cole Bar.

Ten years after Bliss and Faville set out on their design explorations from San Francisco, Simon Benson, a Portland, Oregon, lumber baron, sent his architect, A. E. Doyle, on a countrywide investigation of the best hotel styles and features to incorporate into his eponymous grand hotel at Portland's commercial and cultural center. Although today the Benson's brochure states that its lobby has an "ambiance quite unlike any other hotel," it was, in fact, modeled after the

(Above) Gold Corinthian capitals proudly
define the venerable Westin St. Francis lobby
in San Francisco. The reddish-gold palette
warms the interior; the marble columns and
floors convey its grandeur. The chandelier and
bouquet of fresh flowers are de rigueur.
Although now mainly used as a foyer, there is
usually some seating, which was removed for
this picture. The Compass Rose Bar is up a
few steps from the lobby. (Westin St. Francis)

(Left) San Francisco's Westin St. Francis:
"Meet me under the clock." (Westin St. Francis)

(Opposite, above left) When the Westin St.
Francis first opened, Victorian clutter was in
vogue. Surfaces incorporate pattern and
detail woven together. Massive and dark,
furnishings and finishes visually break up the
room typified by the scattered oriental rugs
and elaborately framed wall panel paintings.
The coffered ceiling and richly veined
columns meld with all surfaces, only
emerging as distinct design features as the rest
of the rooms simplify. The lobby and its
furnishings contrast a lived-in feeling with a
public scale. (Westin St. Francis)

(Opposite, above right) San Francisco's
Westin St. Francis: Keeping up with the
times, the lobby strove for the modern with
hard surfaces, futuristic fixtures, and curved
lines in the late fifties and early sixties. (Westin
St. Francis)

(Opposite, below) San Francisco's Westin St.
Francis: Businesslike chairs and wall-to-wall
carpet visually unify the room as postwar
modernity creeps in. As the furniture and
wall surfaces simplify, the chandeliers become
more ornate. (Westin St. Francis)

(Left) The Westin St. Francis's Compass Rose is a convenient San Franciscan meeting place for travelers and locals alike. An eclectic array of decoration and objects creates interest and activity within the strong structure of fluted columns (which date from its opening), painted beamed ceilings, and wood-paneled walls. A successful juxtaposition of scale arises between the architectural features of the large room and the smaller furnishings and decor. Jade dragon table pedestals, Burmese screens, and Japanese curtains imbue the room with a slight exoticism which is intensified by the warm red and gold color scheme. During the popular afternoon tea, arched windows allow in light and the visual bustle of the city. The room also looks out on the lobby below. It's hard to believe that this is the same space as the Patent Leather Bar, which spent much energy extolling the dark and the artificial.
(Westin St. Francis)

(Page 78) The Westin St. Francis's Patent Leather Bar and Orchid Room (1939): For one of the most extravagant repeal cocktail lounges, architect Timothy Pflueger designed a completely interior room, sealing the windows to create an environment all its own. Black quilted patent leather, Lucite ceilings, mirrors, and the reflective serpentine bar create a cocoon. A self-professed stage set, lighting above the ceiling changed colors at frequent intervals for dramatic effect. (Westin St. Francis)

(Page 79) Post-Prohibition hotel bars took it upon themselves to appeal to women, trying to avoid becoming smoky male enclaves. Women in furs were, presumably, the antithesis.
(Westin St. Francis)

(Left) New York's St. Regis: This tiny room off the lobby corridor beckons you to step inside and become part of its tableau vivant. Pretend you're spending at least one teatime in someone's (at least a marquise) well-appointed chateau. The dark, rich colors of the walls, tapestry upholstery, and serious art contrast with the lightness and openness of the Astor Court just outside its doorway. The room is almost too perfect, implying a roped-off entrance as if a museum model room. (Eleanor Lambert Ltd.)

(Below) The St. Regis lobby, looking up into the Astor Court. (Eleanor Lambert Ltd.)

(Left) The Astor Court at the St. Regis Hotel, New York: The creams and golds convey French luxury reflecting the St. Regis's history. This lobby is one of the few that benefit from a light color scheme, which, in America at least, seems to cheapen larger spaces. Here, however, it communicates elegance not ersatz images of wealth. The proportions of the spaces, change of levels, and visual (and aural, if the piano is being played) axis all serve to enliven the formal space. The pastel murals complete the fantasy. (Brennan Beer Gorman/Architects)

The massive (and masculine) structure constitutes a formidable presence at the Benson Hotel in Portland, Oregon. The lobby has no one particular focus, but simply and directly lays out its functions in a matter-of-fact and, despite its rich materials, informal way. The high, white plaster ceiling is elaborately detailed with Corinthian moldings and coffers inlaid with rosettes, all lightly whipped together, like meringue. This delicacy of ornamentation contrasts with the square, dark, simple Ionic columns supporting it. (Dick Busher/Benson Hotel)

Portland's Benson Hotel: The fireplace, universally a symbol of warmth and welcome, anchors this corner of the lobby. The requisite grand stairway is gracious, its gentle rise inviting not overbearing. (Mercifully, the upholstery of the chairs has since been changed.) (Benson Hotel)

(Left) Despite being a symbol of southern hospitality and synonymous with Memphis, the Peabody Hotel lobby's scale and decor express all the symptoms of old-world aspirations as seen in the painted beamed ceilings, chandeliers, and two-story formality. (Peabody Hotel)

(Below) The dark burnished wood, rhythmic lighting, and well-placed fronds of the Peabody's Mallards Bar and Grill compose the intimate atmosphere of this informal, but businesslike, bar. (Peabody Hotel)

*(Left) The painted wood-beamed vaulted
ceilings of the Rendezvous Court of the
Biltmore, Los Angeles, create a dramatic
effect. (The Biltmore, Los Angeles)*

*(Above) The Palmer House Hilton in
Chicago is reminiscent of another era when
business and society operated on a grand scale.
(Palmer House)*

Blackstone Hotel in Chicago. The 1908 Blackstone Hotel by Marshall & Fox, architects, with its dark wood-paneled walls and elaborate plaster ceiling, was the epitome of the grand and gracious urban hotel in its day.

Both hotels are on the National Register of Historic Places; the Blackstone Hotel, however, is in great need of renovation. The Benson Hotel has had a much more pampered past. Its owners have carefully maintained the aura and reality of the grand lobby in which European splendor is translated into a solid American western presence. The requisite imported materials—fine Austrian chandeliers, Italian marble floors, and oriental rugs, along with dark walnut paneling—are combined in a straightforward and accessible fashion. (Evidently, the architect deemed the native Douglas firs inelegant compared to wood from Circassia in Russia.) The lobby is grand in scale and comfortable in feeling, the perfect combination for the classic center for conducting business in Portland.

For old-world grandeur designed to impress, if only from its scale, Chicago's Palmer House Hilton is hard to surpass. Built in 1925, this third incarnation of the hotel synonymous with the Windy City since 1871 boasts of a main lobby that could be mistaken in size and decoration for a ballroom in Versailles. The two-story room is topped with a ceiling mural of Greek myths painted in a romantic style.

RENOVATION AND RESTORATION

The importance of the hotel renovation and restoration category lies in recent history. The hotels in this group, returned to their original grandeur within the past ten years, were rescued after being in disrepair or even closed for many years. As a testament to the durability of their designs, these hotels have since regained their place in the urban fabric. In restoration, they reprise the role they played in their heyday as centers of urbaneness and of social and business activity.

Rich in local history and often synonymous with the cities themselves, these hotels continue to assume important roles. Not only do they lend continuity to the streetscape, their showcase grand interior spaces re-create glimpses of our past and provide a vital link in local history. These hotels are where people returned year after year, where weddings of successive generations took place, where congratulatory dinners were held, where visiting diplomats and celebrities entertained.

Although specifics differ, the stories behind restored hotels are surprisingly similar in history and local importance as well as in renovation sagas. Throughout America, their demise usually coincided with the decline in importance of center cities around the midsixties. Fewer people came to the city, reducing hotel patronage. Some hotels began to look old and tired. Keeping pace with technological advances and life safety-code requirements entailed large infusions of money. Often, the original number of rooms could not sustain economic viability, necessitating the addition of either more hotel rooms or an office tower to provide other sources of income. Many hotels declared bankruptcy. Renovation required the financial backing and cooperation of owners, banks, and governmental and nonprofit agencies.

In restoring a building that has performed many roles over a period of 50 to 100 years, the question of what constitutes an accurate renovation (or even if that is desirable) usually arises. In restoring hotel lobbies and other public rooms, the job is yet more complex. Hotels continually changed with the times. More important, hotel lobbies are impressions. Their symbols, not the accuracy of their details, speak to us. The restorer must balance what is historically correct with what appears correct or feels right to the modern eye.

Perhaps one of the most difficult, and ultimately most successful, renovations is the Willard Inter-Continental Hotel in Washington, D.C. This hotel was designed in 1901 by Henry Janeway Hardenbergh, the architect of the original Waldorf-Astoria (1890–1893) and the Plaza Hotel (1907). Consistent with the standard history of hotels, this building was not the first Willard at its location but the last one in a long line of expansions and improvements. The pivotal role it played in the capital's social and political life prompted Nathaniel Hawthorne to write during the Civil War that the Willard "more justly could be called the center of Washington and the Union than either the Capitol or the White House or the State Department."[3]

The lobby itself was a place of influence, welcoming presidents, elected officials, dignitaries, and hangers-on. President U. S. Grant, accustomed to relaxing in the lobby when he was a general during the Civil War, continued this practice on assuming presidential office. Knowing that he could be found there, influence peddlers and those pleading various causes tried to gain access to him. In a most likely apocryphal story, Grant is said to have labeled them "lobbyists."

Hardenbergh drew upon the history of the Willard and designed its new building to accentuate and reinforce those vital scenes taking place in its public rooms by creating two lobbies, Peacock Alley (see Chapter 2) and the Round Robin Bar. Its Peacock Alley (the second such corridor designed by Hardenbergh, the first being in the original Waldorf) was a street-length corridor stretching between the two lobbies intended solely for social strutting. It was the place in Washington to see and be seen.

Rich history and magnificent spaces could not, however, compensate for minimal maintenance and deteriorating neighborhoods. The Willard closed in 1968. After many false starts and near demolition, the hotel finally reopened in 1986. Its renovation posed interesting questions concerning historical renovation and the role of grand public spaces.

After years of disuse, including 17 years of vacancy and abandonment, very little of the hotel had not been destroyed or seriously compromised. All rooms as well as structural and mechanical systems required complete overhaul. Being on the National Register of Historic Places imposed certain requirements on exterior repair and expansion. The Pennsylvania Avenue Development Corporation (PADC), a federal agency created by Congress, bought the property to revitalize the urban link between the White House and the Capitol.

Historic restoration of the interior was confined to major public spaces: main lobby, Peacock Alley, and the F Street Lobby (along with a function room and restaurant). These public rooms were re-created to appear as they did circa the 1901 opening rather than any intermediate renovations and refurbishments,

(Above) Symmetrical formality marks the ornate lobby of the Seelbach Hotel in Louisville, Kentucky. (Seelbach Hotel)

(Right) Classical proportions and symmetry are evident in this view of the Willard Inter-Continental Hotel in Washington, D.C. Arches, engaged columns with gilded capitals, patterned ceiling molding, and other architectural details visually activate the walls of the room. The chandeliers, replicas of the originals, are composed of five glass globes supported by arched bronze female figures. Since turn-of-the-century lighting levels were much lower than today's, additional light sources, such as down lighting within the ceiling decoration, have been installed. Despite their subject matter, they are among the most restrained chandeliers in hotels today, an insertion of the art nouveau spirit within the Victorian interior. (Willard Inter-Continental Hotel)

(Above) The furniture centerpiece of the Willard Inter-Continental's lobby is a circular, tufted velvet settee, called a roundabout or pouf, popular at the time the hotel was built. The pouf has made a comeback at the end of this century and can be seen in many hotels today as the hallmark of old-world style. (Willard Inter-Continental Hotel)

(Right) The grandeur, symmetry, and solidness of the room is echoed in the concierge desk, which was modeled after the original front desk. Its massiveness recalls architecture more than furniture. (Willard Inter-Continental Hotel)

(Below) Except during Prohibition, the Round Robin Bar has long been a premier Washington location for the press, politicians, and poseurs. In designing the 1901 building, Hardenbergh was sure to include this pre-Civil War institution, home to both the mint julep (1850) and the first Gridiron Club presidential dinner (1885). Because of the lack of accurate documentation, this room was not historically reconstructed. Dark wood and green felt walls and drapes team up with a dark wood bar and brass railings to achieve a prototypical masculine atmosphere. It is unusual to see the colors and new materials so clearly in such a room since they are most often preserved under a century of cigar and cigarette smoke. The circular bronze chandelier above the bar was at one time illuminated by gas. (Willard Inter-Continental Hotel)

which were many. The interior was renowned for its intricate plaster work, carved ceilings, elaborate mosaic marble tile floors, and chandeliers. Many of the finishes and furnishings are either restorations or reproductions of what was actually at the Willard at the turn of the century or are typical of that period's Beaux-Arts or French Renaissance style. The overall effect is one of grandeur and warmth, which is reinforced by the color palette of soft yellows and oranges.

The main lobby's magnificent scale and proportions (today perhaps only rivaled by Chicago's Palmer House Hilton and Richmond's Jefferson) are visions of another era. The size and height of the room, however, do not intimidate, but appear gracious. Architecturally, the impressively large space is, through details, artfully translated into a comfortable room of comprehensible proportions. Surface pattern and combinations of materials create controlled clutter. Elaborate carvings and moldings activate wall surfaces. One-story columns, second-floor arches, and wainscoting on the perimeter walls of the lobby further reduce the scale. Patterned mosaics add depth and interest to floors, over which are strewn flowered carpets. The carpets, in turn, define smaller areas within the room, creating vignettes for either sitting, waiting, or conducting business, and in effect, visually make the room more accessible and usable.

What is genuine and what is fake are not clear or consistent, neither in 1901 nor now. For example, the building's structural steel frame placed steel and plaster columns in the main lobby. Evidently too austere for turn-of-the-century taste, the columns were finished with scagliola, a nineteenth-century handcrafted finish that imitates marble by impregnating plaster with color and silk threads.[4]

The proliferation of large live flower arrangements and areca palms brings further life to the room. Flowers and plants were indispensable during Victorian times and, as can be seen in many pictures in this book, they are today as well.

Further south, on a smaller scale in a smaller capital, the same story unfolded. In 1908, Little Rock welcomed the second incarnation of the Capital Hotel, advertised as the largest lobby in the region (the promoters conveniently ignored the Willard and the Jefferson). At this transition, "The Arkansaw Traveler" remarked upon the importance and connection of the hotel with the public life of the city since 1877:

> ... within its walls had been settled the destinies of almost every politician that has sought office in Arkansas during the past 40 years. If walls had mouths as well as ears, those of the old Capital hotel could tell tales which would be more interesting than any history ever written. From rooms in the Capital have been pulled wires which have elected governors, presidents of the Senate, and speakers of the House of Representatives.

The usual superlatives emanated from the owners and patrons alike. With evidently no small plans in mind, the owners commissioned the architect of the then-new state capitol to design its sister center of power. To herald its importance, the entrance was accentuated by a two-story porch attached to its Italianate cast-iron facade. It continued its prominent role until the postwar years when it slid into severe ruin.

Rescued after many years of neglect capped by five years of actual closure, the Capital Hotel reopened in December 1983 to resemble its 1908 version. For all its purported largeness, the two-story lobby is notable for its manageable proportions. Echoing its exterior, superimposed orders define the two-story atrium and visually break down the scale of the room. Rather than two-story columns unifying and enlarging the atrium, stately, solid one-story columns support the beamed mezzanine floor above, while true to the classical orders, arches rhythmically spring from the second-story Ionic columns. The atrium is rich with small details that make its refinement accessible, such as the brackets and moldings decorating the floor entablature.

Its materials approximate the Willard's, but its scale and color palette produce a completely different effect. Mosaic tile floors, marble walls and stairs, and scagliola columns comprise the lobby's materials. The cool whites and creams of the marble of the Capital Hotel are bathed with the light from the stained-glass skylight.

Milwaukee was where Guido Pfister made his fortune after emigrating from Germany, and in the democratic tradition of his adopted country, he built a grand hotel in the belief that American luxury should not be restricted by class. In 1893, the Pfister Hotel opened its doors. Designed by H. C. Koch and J. J. Esser, architects of Milwaukee's City Hall, and at a cost greater than that civic structure, the Pfister was a marvel of modern conveniences and extravagances. To celebrate its centennial, the lobby's luxurious accommodation was restored.

In continuous operation for over 100 years, the Pfister Hotel's story presents no rising phoenixes nor perilous last-minute deliverance from destruction. Its renovation does, however, typify the removal of decades-old accumulation of finishes and plan changes. In the process, as marble columns emerged from under wallpaper and ornamentation liberated from behind plasterboard, the original use of the lobby—as the meeting place of old Milwaukee—returned.

Over the years, the ground floor lobby was divided into smaller rooms to accommodate cafes and other areas. With period photographs as a guide, renovation brought back the original salon feeling to the lobby. To complete this vignette, a lobby focal point, an elaborate fireplace that disappeared during a previous modernization, was uncovered. The Pfister Hotel lobby has once again become a destination.

Although this is a renovation that aimed to be historically accurate, restoration of the hotel's barrel vault skylight was not feasible. Taking artistic license, the designers painted the vault with a mural of the sky, complete with clouds and putti. This lends the necessary lightness and lightheartedness to what, for all its good materials, is a heavy, serious room.

Not all hotels that delve into historicism get inspiration from Europe. There are a few that wander further afield, rakishly mixing exoticism and eclecticism. Freed from the restraint of the urban fabric, these hotels generally fall into the regional or urban resort categories. There is, however, a delightful center-city hotel that combines just about every style, making the amalgam its own. It was not built as a hotel at all, but as an athletic club in the fateful year of 1929. The Hotel Inter-Continental Chicago started as the Medinah Athletic Club, a Shriner men's club. Original imagery ranged from neo-Egyptian bas-reliefs on the exterior to Celtic, Mesopotamian, and Assyrian motifs on the interior.

(Above, left) Before the Capital Hotel was restored in 1983, it had been closed for over 6 years and down on its luck even longer. Although time and weather have evidently taken their toll, the proud structure and atrium are striking.
(Cromwell Architects Engineers)

(Above, right) Smaller scale furniture arrangements make the meeting rooms popular. (Cromwell Architects Engineers)

(Right) The cool palette of the permanent interior finishes of the marble and tile are reiterated in the furnishings and carpet.
(Cromwell Architects Engineers)

(Opposite, above) The terra cotta fireplace reflects the arches on the exterior and has once again become a focal point of the lobby.
(Pfister Hotel/Ellingsen/Sprecher)

(Opposite, below) As solid as its midwestern heritage, the Pfister Hotel's lobby conveys down-to-earth luxury as its square columns accept their heavy load. The barrel vault provides the necessary airiness. The functions of the lobby are clearly delineated and gracefully zoned. Circulation and main desk area are separate and lit more dramatically than the more intimate, low-ceiling salon area. The new furniture layout reflects a living-room feeling. (Pfister Hotel/Ellingsen/Sprecher)

This extravagance could not endure through the Depression, and the building closed its doors after five years of operation. Ten years later, it was transformed into a hotel, only to close again in 1986. Reopened under new management in 1989 after a thoughtful and spirited renovation, the hotel is a feast of decoration and ornament. Although the entrance is merely a foyer, small in plan and lacking a place for one to rest, its sense of entry and welcome is grand and expansive.

THE LIVING ROOM

Grand proportions and huge rooms are not prerequisites for old-world luxury. The living-room lobby, while not as public as the grand hotel, provides wonderful respite from the urban pace. This type of lobby asks to be used and enjoyed. No peacock alleys here. Comfort of the homey sort connotes a certain level of clutter and eclecticism, an ease of mixing styles and colors.

Despite its name, the Majestic Hotel in the Pacific Heights neighborhood of San Francisco is a small hotel, built in 1902 in an Edwardian style. The antique-strewn lobby and bar contain furniture, fixtures, and objets d'art from all over the world without regard to country or century, but with a result of charming all visitors. It is just like walking into someone's house, someone who happened to have impeccable taste and had traveled the world collecting special fixtures and furniture.

THE URBAN RESORT

Another slightly less formal version of old-world elegance can be found in the urban resort. Tracing its beginnings to the resort hotel, most of these hotels were originally built as country refuges. The world has changed around them: Urban growth reached their doors, and their clientele expanded with the times.

The heyday of the country refuge—the large, usually rambling, resort far from urban centers—spanned the mid-1800s through the early 1900s. Families migrated en masse during summer months to seek relief from urban weather and disease, pursuing pleasure. This clientele searched for a change of pace and venue in hopes of finding renewed health as well as kindred souls in terms of class and tastes (whether real or aspired). Many of these resorts were exclusive and restrictive, affording to those admitted the opportunity to see and, perhaps, imitate the lifestyles of famous personalities and political leaders.[5]

These resorts were usually located to take advantage of natural features or beauty such as springs, mountains, or the seashore. When they were built, they were remote and difficult to reach, requiring days of travel by railroad or stage. Isolated, these hotels reinforced an aura of exclusivity and privacy. No matter how distant from society, however, these resorts were up to date in terms of the services, conveniences, and amenities provided. As with all hotels, modern comforts and old-world aesthetics peacefully coexisted.

Architectural styles and images were wide-ranging and flamboyant. These hotels spread horizontally over unlimited acres and appropriated, exaggerated, and improvised on any and all architectural styles. These styles reflected the tastes of owners or the imagination of architects, not the actual location or region.

In search of privacy and change from their urban lifestyle, the guests did not demand that the lobbies and public rooms be the stages for the urban theatrics of people watching. These lobbies were, however, pivotal social gathering spots. Seldom solely interior spaces, they spilled out onto commodious porches and vast manicured lawns, sited to focus on the mountains, ocean, or wilderness beyond.

Today, many of these resorts have closed. Those that have survived have redefined themselves in light of changing circumstances. No longer isolated geographically as development has extended to meet them, country refuges have transformed themselves into the urban resort. The Hotel Del Coronado, or The Del as it's known locally, typifies the new urban resort. Over a hundred years ago, San Diego and an adjacent island, Coronado, were sparsely inhabited. When the transcontinental railroad reached the Pacific Ocean, entrepreneurs developed Coronado as a new town, a destination for winter-weary easterners. Complete with the most up-to-date comforts and services, but separated from the world around it, the hotel took command of its beautiful setting and climate.

James and Merritt Reid, architect brothers from Indiana, designed a rambling Queen Anne Victorian wood-framed structure within sight of the Mexican border. The resort hotel had this spit of sand called the Silver Strand all to itself. Although the hotel was located in the wilderness, roughing it was out of the question. It supported itself with its own kiln, power plant, and all other required facilities. Isolation did not equate with backwardness: Thomas Edison supervised the installation of electricity; furniture, tableware, and fittings were all imported from Europe. The town has since surrounded the hotel: Tall condominiums dwarf the hotel in height but definitely not in spirit.

Rejecting sea, sand, and Mexican allusions, the lobby re-creates a small English world. No ersatz Spanish details or hints of stucco mar the fantasy. Dark polished wood, deep-colored rugs, and European furniture grace the rooms. Blinding bright sunlight bathes the grounds and building; cool darkness rules the lobby, an often welcome contrast and relief in a part of the country where shelter from the sun is often sought.

The entire main floor and grounds are given over to public spaces, arenas for sustaining social activity or finding privacy during long stays. Lobbies, nooks, and verandas are settings for strutting, viewing the sea, or just sitting. For a sheltered sunlit experience, an exterior courtyard plays the lobby's counterpart. This outdoor room, surrounded on all sides by the wings of the hotel, is just a step outside the lobby. Originally a tropical garden, it is now a quiet retreat.

While originally a destination resort, The Del now fulfills that role as well as that of urban resort. Its lobby is now the stopping off point for tourists, locals, and local social events as well as home to resort goers. The spaces are flexible enough to adapt to many uses. Its site, with its large expanse of beach, will never go out of style.

(Opposite, above left) The foyer and stair at the Hotel Inter-Continental in Chicago. (Inter-Continental Hotel, Chicago)

(Opposite, above right) The mahogany, horseshoe-shaped bar first did duty in a Paris bistro. (Majestic Hotel)

(Opposite, below) The feeling of the Majestic Hotel's lobby derives from the furniture and decoration as opposed to the architecture or proportions. Although the lobby is small, there are several seating areas to accommodate different groupings simultaneously, especially with the creation of a semiseparate room up the stairs. The cream-colored walls with gray-blue trim are complemented by the muted red in the carpet and furnishings. No two items are identical, yet they all seem to go together. Note the two different chandeliers. (Majestic Hotel)

(Above, left) The two-story oak lobby of the Four Seasons Olympic Hotel in Seattle is larger than the Majestic Hotel and lays claim to a more formal living-room feeling. (Four Seasons Olympic Hotel)

(Above, and left) Lobby living room and French room bar: Both these wood-paneled public rooms of the Adolphus Hotel in Dallas are explorations of bucolic fantasies. These sitting rooms evoke a landed estate, most likely in England. (The Adolphus Hotel)

(Above) The dark wood interior and heavy chandeliers testify to the Hotel Del Coronado's European Victorian heritage. From this room it is difficult to imagine that Mexico and the beach are just yards away.
(Hotel del Coronado)

(Above, right) This is an early view from a postcard of the dining room, which spans its 66-ft width without columns. The exposed vaulted ceiling is constructed from sugar pine and fastened by wooden pegs, not nails. The room has been named the Crown Room after the crown-shaped chandeliers designed by Frank Baum, author of The Wizard of Oz.
(Hotel del Coronado)

(Below, right) The Crown Room today.
(Hotel del Coronado)

(Inset) Old photograph of the courtyard showing a fountain and statue (a replica of an original gazebo is in the center of the courtyard now). The courtyard functions as an outdoor room, completely enclosed by the hotel wings. Imported exotic tropical plants fill the grounds. (Hotel del Coronado)

The Dining Room, Coronado Hotel, Coronado, Cal.

The Fountain, Court Yard,
Hotel Coronado,
Coronado, Cal.

Chapter 6

DESIGNER VISIONS

D ESIGNER-VISION hotel lobbies are rarities. They create a buzz when they open because their portrayal of elegance obviously veers from the traditional. Their design does not refer to other times or other places but to themselves or even their designers. They share distinctiveness rather than a consistent trend. Ostensibly lacking a unified style, they are, notwithstanding insistent individuality and resistance of categorization, modern.

Two eras conducive to designer-vision hotels have been the late 1920s and the 1980s. Several similarities connect the two. Commercial and public building booms flourished during both eras, stimulating a spirit of design experimentation. At the same time, prevailing concepts of modern floundered, prompting a search for progressive aesthetics that spoke directly to the times. In both eras, design inquiries were international in scope and in influence; the exchange and cross-fertilization of ideas were commonplace.

The term *Art Deco* derives from the highly influential *Exposition des Arts Décoratifs et Industriels Modernes* held in Paris in 1925. The quest for modern eclipsed all other concerns. The show's requirements mandated that all submissions be original; designs imitating popular styles or reeking of historicism were inadmissible. The resulting style, however eclectic and varied in its sources, combined appealing geometric ornament with lavish and opulent colors and materials. Art Deco quickly became marketable, a modern style accessible to the general public. Evidently, Art Deco's rich decoration and ornament were more attractive and compelling than designs emanating from other contemporaneous modern movements such as the Bauhaus, whose intellectual exhortations for simplification were spurned.

Silver chaise from the Paramount, New York.
(Tom Vack/Nancy Assuncao Associates)

Architects and interior designers quickly seized upon the commercial possibilities of Art Deco. Converts were many, all spreading word of this new style. Designs were altered in midproject and new plans drawn as geometric ornament was applied and buildings were bedecked in Art Deco fashion. In 1928, two New York department stores, Macy's and Lord & Taylor, separately showcased new designs of furniture and objects. One year later, the Metropolitan Museum of Art in New York mounted its Art Deco show.

Art Deco was urban and theatrical, a combination ripe for hotel exploitation. Many hotels were built in the late 1920s and, as a result, have some Art Deco detail or motifs. Unfortunately, most existing Art Deco hotel interiors no longer exist. The most famous Art Deco hotel is the second (and current) Waldorf-Astoria Hotel in New York, designed by Schultze and Weaver in 1929–1931. Its sumptuousness paradoxically heralded the Depression. Its Art Deco heritage remains only on its exterior and in its main lobby, renovations having hidden or deemphasized many of the original Art Deco interior details.

The most complete intact Art Deco hotel in America today is the Omni Netherland Plaza in Cincinnati, designed in 1931 by Walter W. Ahlschlager (who also was responsible for the Hotel Inter-Continental in Chicago, 1929) and George Unger, a theater designer. As ornate as the Waldorf-Astoria Hotel is restrained, the Omni Netherland Plaza showcases a sophisticated designer's vision, incorporating such eclectic influences as New York skyscraper, French Art Deco, Egyptian allusions, as well as local motifs and exotic materials. Restored by Richard Rauh & Associates, Ltd. Architects, the hotel's details, ornament, and public spaces once again shine.[1]

This hotel is part of a large, mixed-use development composed of three towers—hotel, offices, and parking—sitting atop a three-story retail base.[2] Entrance to the hotel is complex and accessible from several levels: streets, retail arcade, and city skywalk. Unlike other mall hotels, the street entrance is not merely an austere elevator lobby but the starting point of a stately procession that unifies these potentially confusing and conflicting entries. Starting with a grand staircase at street level, the three-story lobby is visually and physically connected by a vertical spiral of public spaces.

Visual unity is also achieved through attention to detail. Luxury is everywhere. Contrasting with black Italian marble and Brazilian rosewood are gilded column capitals and ornate light fixtures. Warm colors in the artwork and furnishings accentuate the elegance. Elaborate and complex detailing animates every surface. The interior of the Omni Netherland Plaza is a distinctly French version of Art Deco. In fact, many of the fixtures and ornaments seen in railings, grilles, and ceilings were ordered directly from the catalogue of the 1925 Paris exhibition.

At the same time as the Omni Netherland Plaza was changing Cincinnati's skyline, further west, in the desert bordering Phoenix, Frank Lloyd Wright and Albert Chase McArthur were integrating the Arizona Biltmore with its surrounding landscape.[3] Originally designed to be a playground for the social elite, the Arizona Biltmore has expanded its clientele with the times. Although more a destination resort and conference center than an urban retreat, the designer's vision it represents cannot be omitted from any book about hotels.

Made from precast concrete blocks molded on site, the materials, color, and massing are reminiscent of the desert and mountains just outside the hotel windows, integrating the building with its environment. Forms molded into the blocks simultaneously recall desert plant forms as well as abstract geometric motifs popular in the 1920s.

The 250-ft-long lobby is the heart of the hotel, the site of the main promenade and lounge seating as well as necessary hotel functions such as registration. The lobby's design grows out of the building's architecture; it is not applied or separate. The same structural exterior concrete blocks are exposed throughout, further relating the building's interior to its surroundings. These blocks provide scale, proportion, and continuity to the interior public spaces. The lighting—opaque glass blocks integrated into the block wall system—is placed to provide not only illumination but decoration and rhythm to the lobby.

The overall coloring of the hotel lobby is the earthy gray-beige of the unpainted concrete blocks. The floors were originally stained green but have since been carpeted in a pattern originally designed for Wright's Imperial Hotel in Tokyo. Further contributing to the warmth of the lobby is the gold leaf of the ceiling.

The late 1980s witnessed a spurt in hotel design exploration similar in intent to the late 1920s: the search for a modern that is both comfortable and extraordinary. Disdaining the cliché and the usual, these hotels represent cutting-edge design. Cutting-edge design is audacious. It risks offense. Its goals and images, however, are not shared by all. Too modern, off-putting, or self-indulgent for some, yet exciting, sophisticated, and amusing for others, this design extracts extreme reactions. Its strength, then, is often its very problem. Although provocation attracts as well as repels, few hotel owners are willing to experiment, knowing that the downside of this design is its staying power, or rather the ability of the design to stay powerful.

(Above) Omni Netherland Plaza: Named after the original in Louis XIV's Versailles, this Hall of Mirrors is a confection of light and metal, all reflected in amber mirrors. Filigree metalwork of the balustrade combines bronze and nickel-silver, Art Deco's favorites to replicate gold and silver. The garland frieze at the ceiling unifies the room. (© 1988 Norman McGrath/Richard Rauh & Associates)

(Left) Omni Netherland Plaza: Combining Egyptian and French influences, seahorses sporting lotus leaf lights guard a fountain topped by a ram's head, all molded at Cincinnati's own Rookwood Pottery. This serves as the entry to the former dining room, now a function room. (© 1988 Norman McGrath/Richard Rauh & Associates)

New York has recently seen the revival of the urban hotel that sets out to be grand as well as individual. In a design world that is normally self-conscious, these cutting-edge design hotels stand out as being totally self-possessed. Refusing to meet an established standard of elegance, they invent their own definitions of the good life. In the sociology of hotels, cutting-edge design does not cater to the bourgeois or to those who think of themselves as such. Writers, actors, designers are generally the target audience. These are, however, notoriously fickle groups, quick to leave for the next new scene.

Chief among this new group are the Royalton (see Chapter 4) and the Paramount Hotel, both successful exercises in renovation as transformation and both designed by Philippe Starck and owned by Ian Schrager. Although the Paramount's columnless two-story lobby is small in plan, it is large in spirit. Its self-conscious stage set waits for the play to begin. The square-plan lobby is a stylized living room, complete with checkerboard area rug, conversation groupings, little table lamps, and 1940s black rotary-dial house phones. The gray walls act as a neutral scrim against which colorful furniture and spots of light play. The sculptured stair leading to the second floor simultaneously appears massive and floating, the transparent glass rail invisible against the white-gold-leaf backdrop wall.

Seeing and being seen are given equal weight. Tables in the second floor restaurant are framed by openings in the lobby's walls, participating in the space beneath: the perfect place to be on display and to look upon the happenings below.

The Paramount's sophistication is on a small scale. The Four Seasons Hotel in New York, recently designed by Pei Cobb Freed & Partners Architects (with interiors by Chhada, Siembieda & Partners), unabashedly presents modern on a public scale. This hotel takes its civic role seriously. Its strong volumes and formal plan recall our grander urban traditions. Its design relies on impeccably detailed materials and elegantly proportioned spaces, not decoration.

The foyer sets the tone boldly and without frills. The hard surfaces of marble and limestone are seamlessly intertwined and contrasted with polished wood and translucent onyx. Architecture, not appliqué, holds forth. Surfaces are smooth and clean. Art Deco inspired, ornament stems from the use of materials as seen in the black marble floor inset with light marble in a weblike design. (The floor design invokes the piazza of Michelangelo's Campidoglio in Rome; the referenced monumentality is presumably intentional.)

From the austere symmetrical foyer to the softly upholstered lobby lounges and then to the upstairs piano bar, the Four Seasons Hotel's progression of public spaces is as carefully programmed as a gavotte. The plan of the public areas is unremittingly axial (but not direct), leading one through three distinct floor levels starting from the grand foyer and ending with a grand piano. The promenade is achieved in stages, with linear passage being blocked at the end of each level, forcing a change in direction and vista. Spaces are discovered incrementally by walking around before rising to another level. The ceiling elevation, however, remains static, so that the procession is through a simple, though monumental, spatial volume.

As vertical and voluminous as the Four Seasons Hotel is, the Hotel Nikko at Beverly Hills is horizontal and sprawling. This addition to the Japanese hotel chain is a study of contrasts and contradictions; its lobby simultaneously suggests Japan and Los Angeles. Whatever its pedigree, high design is its drama. Every detail is crisp and clear. Its understated elegance combines modernity with tradition.

The Hotel Nikko's lobby design is a series of paradoxes. The sense of grandeur is achieved not through height but from distance. Its horizontal vistas are as endless as freeways but are as calming and controlled as a Japanese garden. With a sure sense of proportion and detail, the uniform ceiling height avoids conveying claustrophobia as so often happens in new buildings. Its uncluttered, refined style is neither cold nor harsh but as welcoming and comfortable as a living room.

Juxtapositions abound: Hard marble surfaces abut soft leather furniture; the nature contrasts with the artificial. The lobby is organized around a skylit sculpture and rock garden, introducing nature into the room. A fountain provides a murmur of sound, its water skimming over the shiny marble base. At the perimeter, walls of shoji-type grids define alcoves or niches off the main room for more private groupings.

*(Above) The Arizona Biltmore's main lobby
forms a 250-ft-long promenade. Lighting
blocks integrated within the structure provide
the room with rhythm and grace.*
(Arizona Biltmore)

*(Right) Arts and Crafts chairs and Art Deco-
inspired light fixtures adorn the lobby lounge.*
(Arizona Biltmore)

*(Left) The living-room lobby of the
Paramount Hotel: Food and drinks are served
upstairs. The ground floor is solely devoted to
hotel functions: sitting, meeting, people-
watching, and being observed.*
(Tom Vack/Nancy Assuncao Associates)

*(Above) The Four Seasons's lobby is a 33-ft-
high monument to symmetrical grandeur.
The interior is limestone with an inlaid
backlit onyx ceiling. The rear wall prevents a
simple linear progression, forcing a more
elaborate route to the right or left.*
(Four Seasons Hotel)

(Above) The skylit garden at the center of
the Hotel Nikko at Beverly Hills brings
nature and art into the heart of the lobby.
(Hotel Nikko at Beverly Hills)

(Left) The warm neutrals of the bar are
reflected in the mirror etched with a
reproduction of Kimon Niccolaides's 1920s
drawing of the Central Park carousel. The
furniture and light fixtures subtly evoke the
restrained ornament and elegance of the Art
Deco period. The height of the room conveys
airiness and the formal volumes of the lobby
below. (Four Seasons Hotel)

Chapter 7

REGIONALISM

AMERICAN HOTELS are not as stylistically connected with their locations as with their distinctive roles. As a rule, American public buildings generally reflect what is fashionable in older cities rather than their local or regional architectural character. As a result, hotels consciously refer to or emulate styles prominent in the eastern United States; attempts to prove themselves the equal of or better than any hotel accentuate this tendency. The goal of achieving high levels of luxury, comfort, service, and excellence translates into a design mandate. More loyal to their roles than their region, many hotels are stylistically similar.

But pockets of hotel regional style do exist, reflecting local traditions and influences. Regional style on a public scale is an invented style that adapts a vernacular, often residential, idiom to other uses. Some hotels incorporate these aspects in their architecture; others express local history through design details, furniture, and art.

At the turn of the century, architects and entrepreneurs in California and the Southwest searched for styles that would best represent their regions and visually differentiate themselves from the rest of the country. Their versions of historical design roots successfully took hold, powered by exotic flavor and brimming with apparent authenticity. With an eye toward enticing tourists, many experiments with regional style first occurred in hotels and railroad stations.

The tiled roofs, arches, and bell towers of the California Mission Revival style were the starting, but by no means ending, points of the Mission Inn in Riverside, California. In 1902, Frank Miller, an idiosyncratic collector and eccentric, started expanding the family's hotel. Over a period of thirty years, from 1903 to 1931, his two-story cabin evolved into a block-square fantasy, a melange of Spanish,

La Fonda Hotel, Santa Fe.
(La Fonda Hotel)

Gothic, Moorish, Japanese, and Italian motifs. Stylistic labels, however, fall short of capturing its essence because the Inn is an individualistic vision that, like the Watts Towers, seems to thrive in California, though seldom on such a public scale.

Rising above its neighboring buildings and visible from blocks away, the hotel's mass physically dominates its surroundings. A local landmark, the Mission Inn was the center of social life in Riverside until it closed in 1976. It recently reopened after an extensive renovation directed by the Berkeley firm of ELS/Elbasani & Logan Architects, which included earthquake reinforcement and structural repairs. Although its renaissance is the key (and perhaps only) element in plans for Riverside's downtown revitalization, it is as yet unclear if the Mission Inn alone can accomplish this goal.

The Mission Inn is a triumph of expert showmanship, of an imagined past over reality. In short, for all its foreign references, it is a thoroughly American story. The turn-of-the-century inspiration for the hotel derived from and in turn popularized the Mission Revival style. At a time and in a location that lacked missions and concealed signs of its Hispanic heritage, Miller offered his guests instant history: the impression they were staying in an actual converted mission. In stark contrast to the prototype, his version came with the latest conveniences of fireproof construction, bathrooms, steam heat, and telephone service.

Designed by Los Angeles architect Arthur B. Benton, the Inn extended the full length of a block, its U-shaped building embracing a courtyard. At the street, a stucco arcade punctuated by arched scalloped entrance gates creates the fourth wall of the courtyard. This courtyard entrance, asserting the distinct separation between the hotel and its city, has played the same dual welcome-disassociation role throughout the hotel's many alterations and expansions. Maintaining this separation between the hotel and the town increased in importance as the city grew to meet the edges of the hotel. In addition to the plant-filled courtyard, public gathering places included the main lobby, which originally contained furniture by Gustav Stickley and William Morris scattered about informally. Furthering the hallmarks of the Mission style, the walls were light textured plaster, which contrasted with the dark stained wood of the columns, floors, moldings, and other woodwork.

Miller's itinerary and imagination were the creative points of departure for the Inn's three additional building expansions and innumerable changes. The Spanish-Mediterranean influence, tied to Miller's travels to Spain and his desire to create a center of Spanish art, resulted in the 1914 Spanish Wing designed by Myron B. Hunt. Miller, a compulsive collector, distributed his treasures throughout the public areas and, with larger items such as his bell collection, incorporated them in the architecture. Size was never a restriction; indeed, Miller even imported a complete Mexican altar for the Inn's chapel.

Today, this building of excesses has not one but two arched portals in the approach to its lobby. Entry is a procession. A stuccoed arcade wall, similar to the original, still signals a clear distinction between the street and the hotel, between reality and real-life fantasy. The large courtyard built in 1902 has since been divided to serve three functions. The first is a paved drive bordered by sidewalks catering to both pedestrians and cars. In contrast to this hard surface, a second arched bell gate opens upon a garden courtyard whose lush vegetation offers a welcome reprieve in California's hot desert climate. The other side of the courtyard contains

a large swimming pool, separated from the public entrance by a high wall to maintain privacy. The exterior walls of the building form the interior walls of the courtyard and act as the proscenium through which one enters the hotel itself.

Starting with the entry court, the Inn's public rooms are a labyrinth of indoor and outdoor spaces, enclosed rooms and open courtyards. Stuffed with objects and filled with elaborate detail, this is an extravagant environment with always more to discover, another alcove or statue previously overlooked. The main lobby is a wide corridor connecting the various wings and function rooms as well as a side street entrance.

Perhaps the Mission Revival style hotels built by the Atchison Topeka & Santa Fe Railroad, often in conjunction with the Fred Harvey Company, were the most influential not only because of their numbers but also due to their stylistic consistency. Railroads pushing west attracted tourists who wanted to experience a new world of dramatic landscapes and exotic people, all from a safe and convenient vantage point. The railroad built its stations and accompanying hotels to appeal to travelers lured to the West with the advertising program of "See America First." Romantically interpreting southwestern surroundings and local

Although the Mission Inn has been completely renovated and rebuilt, the main lobby reflects the Mission Revival style of the original first building, the Mission Wing, in which it is located. The deep-toned wood of the beamed ceiling, floors, and columns lend a cool richness to the interior, which is surprisingly simple and devoid of ornamentation. The new carpet depicts all 21 California missions. Mainly a corridor linking all the hotel functions, the lobby contains some seating areas to the left of the carpet. The hotel is trying to replace some of the original furnishings that have been lost or worn out with Mission style pieces to maintain the character of the hotel. The grand staircase creates a graceful backdrop to the registration desk. (Erich Koyama/ELS/Elbasani & Logan Architects)

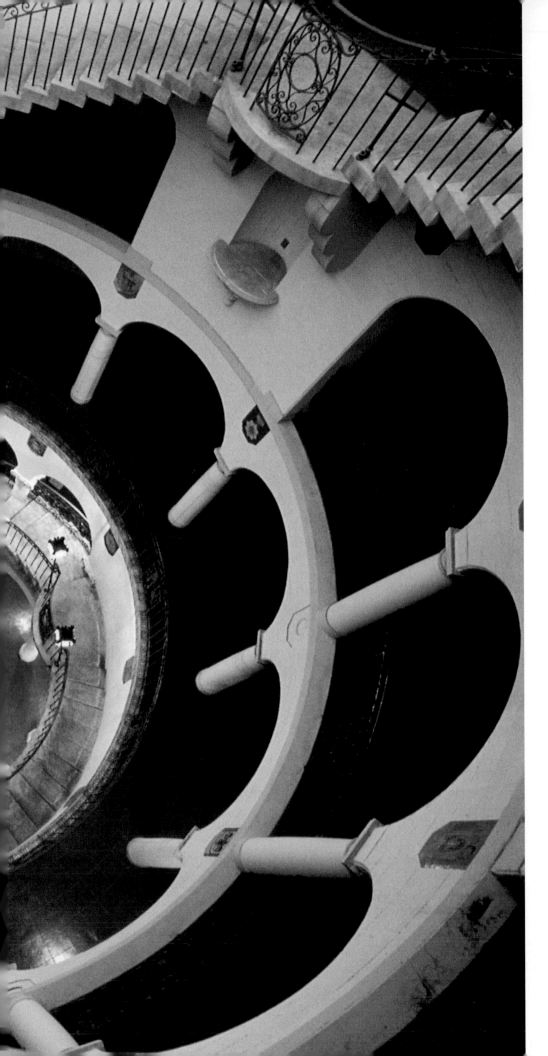

A dramatic shot of the Rotunda of the Mission Inn, built in 1931. The Rotunda continued the idiosyncratic, but heavily Spanish-influenced, style. (Erich Koyama/ELS/Elbasani & Logan Architects)

history with the protective arcades and rusticness of the Mission style, each station along the line re-created and reinforced this consistent theme.

The railroads and the adjacent Fred Harvey Houses offered a total package, complete with transportation, local tours, good food, comfortable rooms, local crafts, and to convey authenticity, a visually different aesthetic from that of the East. These Harvey Houses were among the first to create a style based on the amalgam of Indian and Spanish cultures and, certainly, considering their ubiquity in the West, to popularize it.

One such structure to combine the Indian with Spanish motifs was the Mission style Alvarado Hotel (1902–1970) located at the Albuquerque train station. Although its arcades and pitched roofs proclaimed its mission tradition, the hotel delighted its patrons with its fashionable Indian Room, designed by Mary Colter, who became Fred Harvey's chief architect for subsequent hotels. Decorated with rugs, baskets, and jewelry (all for sale, of course), the Indian Room purported to replicate a pueblo's interior. (Concurrently, thousands of miles away from the source of this inspiration, a bar in New York's Astor Hotel was built around the same theme, just as [in]accurate in its representation but just as well received.)

Well before the rails connected America, there was the Santa Fe Trail, and at the end of the trail, at the plaza in Santa Fe itself, was a hotel. Since 1821, an inn has stood on this site, participating in the fate of its area from the colonial and territorial days through statehood. In 1920, after the demise of the existing inn, the architectural firm of Rapp, Rapp and Henrickson was called upon to design the latest incarnation of La Fonda Hotel. This commission was not idly given.

During the first decade of this century, New Mexican architects searched for an architectural style that would distinguish their region not only from the rest of the country but especially from California and its Spanish-influenced Mission style. To achieve this end, a group of Santa Fe architects selected the Rapp firm to design their building for the 1915 Panama Pacific Exposition in Balboa Park, San Diego. The firm, following strict instructions to design a building in a Santa Fe style, created a building that drew upon the Pueblo traditions of the area.

The design of that New Mexican Building succeeded beyond expectations and defined the style that has become synonymous with that city to this day. Within five years, the Santa Fe Plaza was transformed. Adobe, round log columns, flat roofs, and vigas (extended log roof beams, although often not structural) replaced Greek Revival and colonial details of the Governor's Palace; Spanish street names replaced English; and buildings such as the Museum of Fine Arts, similar to the New Mexican Building at the San Diego exposition, further developed and refined this emerging style. A new hotel, prominently featured on the plaza, secured the stylistic conversion and dominance.

Aesthetically assured but financially shaky, La Fonda was taken over five years later by the Atchison, Topeka and Santa Fe Railroad, which in turn leased it to Fred Harvey in 1926. Working with pueblo themes, La Fonda was expanded and decorated by Mary Colter, building upon her success at the Alvarado Hotel. Combining Spanish and pueblo building motifs, La Fonda represents on a public, and perhaps on a bit too commercial, scale what has become known as the Santa Fe style. Its monochromatic adobe exterior and interiors filled with exposed log beams, clay tile floors, and hand-painted wooden furniture and details are instantly identifiable. Taking advantage of the complexity that the building's different levels provide, public areas incorporate courtyards and roof terraces. Even within the heart of the capital city, the contrast and connection with the dramatic landscape just outside its doorstep are evident. To this day, La Fonda is informal and rustic, although some of the details and furnishings now border on kitsch.

The New Mexican Building, while a stylistic anomaly, was not the only building at the 1915 Panama California Exposition to assert its influence. This exposition was crucial to the development of yet another regional style, the Spanish Colonial Revival. Although the architect in charge, Bertram Grosvenor Goodhue, was from the East, he actively sought inspiration from Mexico as well as the remnants of the local Hispanic culture whose crumbling missions left their imprint on California and the Southwest. Designs shown at the exposition affect the look of that region to this day. The assumption that a regional style existed was so pervasive that a contemporary critic wrote in *The Architectural Record,* "the architectural style selected for the exposition at San Diego is one which is as generally unfamiliar in the country as it is historically and logically appropriate in its use here."

The Spanish Colonial Revival style caught the fancy of southern California. Soon identified with this region, this style exhibits an ease of movement between the indoors and outdoors that is especially felicitous in hotel design in warm climates. Arcades gracefully shelter people from the strong sun. Cooling trees catch the breeze in garden patios creating delightful sitting and dining areas. Sporting much more ornament around their doors and windows than the down-to-earth Mission style, the Spanish Colonial Revival style easily adapted to the carefree image of hotels.

La Jolla's La Valencia, built in 1926, is just such a Mediterranean-inspired hotel that takes advantage of its spectacular setting. La Valencia is a hybrid. It's a resort located in the heart of downtown in a small city, a transition between the street and the Pacific Ocean. Its street frontage, lobby, and bar relate to the town; its patios, rooms, and beach identify with the resort. La Jolla is a town where street activity is lively and strolling is easy. The hotel blends into this atmosphere by maintaining the street line.

La Valencia's front door is at the end of an arcade, a gentle transition between the sidewalk and the hotel. Through the arcade's wide arches, which rest on twisted columns, the trees and flowers of the garden dining patio entice the visitor. Inside, the linear lobby continues its visual lure, culminating in a spectacular ocean view framed by a large window.

Southern California and the Southwest could cite some architectural connections with the Spanish and local Native American cultures that have been reflected in its building designs. Southern Florida, however, had its Mediterranean heritage imposed upon it by northern real estate speculators in search of a marketable commercial identity. Although Ponce de León claimed Florida for Spain in the 1500s, Spanish architectural heritage had been negligible in that state until the late nineteenth century when Henry Flagler, a cofounder of the Standard Oil Company, started developing St. Augustine. Flagler's chosen style, with the help of the temperate climate and quality of light, easily took root and has been considered indigenous ever since.

Flagler was just the first in a long line of real estate promoters who participated and exploited the boom and bust cycles that were and are Florida development. The frenzied economic atmosphere of the 1920s gave rise to George Merrick's City of Coral Gables, a master-planned suburb complete with platted streets and written design guidelines. Spanish-inspired Mediterranean was the chosen style. At the heart of this development was the Coral Gables Biltmore, a massive hotel rising above its neighbors with its 300-ft-high replica of Seville's Giralda Tower. Although miles from the ocean, this exclusive resort gained access to the water by digging a Venetian-style canal from the hotel to Biscayne Bay. It opened in early 1926, the same year as the devastating hurricane that foreshadowed the coming economic bust.

The fateful opening year presaged the uneven history of the Coral Gables Biltmore. After several years of glory, the hotel, as with many other large hotels, was converted into a hospital as part of the war effort, a role the Veteran's Administration continued until 1968. After almost two decades of abandonment, resuscitation efforts succeeded. Reopened for business in 1987, it quickly closed several years later. Since 1992, a new management team has been trying yet again to maintain the hotel.

The Biltmore's original architects, Schultze and Weaver, who also designed many other hotels such as the Los Angeles Biltmore, the Boca Raton Resort, and New York's Hotel Pierre and Waldorf-Astoria, brought their wonderful sense of the variety and grandeur of hotel public spaces to this Biltmore. A melange of Spanish, Moorish, and Beaux-Arts styles, the hotel is marked by stately elegance. The main lobby, on the second floor, is reached by a gently rising road and a ceremonial entrance. The huge lobby contains ribbed groin vaults which spring from two rows of massive columns. Contributing to the magic is the blue background and gold stars of the vaults. The hardness of the lobby's materials is grand and cooling at the same time. The lobby leads to an arcaded patio that overlooks the outdoor cafe below and golf course beyond.

Today's hotel goers search for regional expressions as strongly as seventy years ago. The Governor Hotel in Portland, Oregon, emphasized its regional roots during a recent renovation. At its 1909 opening, the Governor (then called the Seward Hotel) showcased its beautiful exterior terra cotta detailing and burnished its reputation as one of Portland's finest hotels. It was built to take advantage of the prosperity that followed the 1905 Lewis and Clark Exposition, held in Portland to commemorate the 100-year anniversary of the exploration. Today, the Governor's lobby is a comfortable living room with a northwestern theme. Recent artwork commemorates the Lewis and Clark Expedition through large-scaled murals whose four panels tell the tale of the explorers' 2000-mile journey.

Artwork of a different type marks the regional character of the Jefferson in Richmond, Virginia. Designed by Carrère and Hastings in 1895, the hotel has been restored and is now on the National Register of Historic Places and the Virginia Landmarks Register. The Jefferson is an amalgam of styles with the palm court representing Beaux-Arts classicism. The statue of the hotel's namesake dates from its opening and still presides like a national monument under the stained-glass dome of the palm court. Oral tradition has handed down the story that the statue was originally surrounded by water in which live alligators swam.

(Above) Mission Inn: The facade of the 1914 Spanish Wing is the backdrop for the outdoor cafe of the Spanish Patio. Isolated from the rest of the hotel, this space is an oasis within a retreat. (Timothy Hursley/ELS/Elbasani & Logan Architects)

(Left) Mission Inn: As seen at the elevator lobby, the hotel is rich in details of the Mission style. (Erich Koyama/ELS/Elbasani & Logan Architects)

(Left, above) Bell Tower Bar at night.
(La Fonda Hotel)

(Left, below) Even in the heart of the city, terraces, such as the Bell Tower Bar, reaffirm the connection with the landscape beyond. The tile floor and plastered walls contrasting with dark exposed wood beams of La Fonda Hotel are hallmarks of what has come to be known as the Santa Fe style. (La Fonda Hotel)

(Right, above) Vigas flat, corbelled beams and adobe mark the entrance of the Inn of the Anasazi, immediately announcing the hotel's intended connection with its city's visual image. (Inn of the Anasazi)

(Right, middle) Stylistic coherence extends into the comfortable lobby where exposed beams, earth colors, and adobe walls are evident. (Inn of the Anasazi)

(Right, below) The library at the Inn of the Anasazi is a cozy room, easily adapting the hallmarks of the Santa Fe style as its own.
(Inn of the Anasazi)

La Valencia's lobby extends from the street to the Pacific Ocean. In between are the painted wood detailing of the structure, clay tile floors, beautiful mosaics, and the ever-present arches. All recall the heyday of the Spanish Colonial style popular during the 1920s. (La Valencia Hotel)

Massive columns create a stately entrance and lend a sense of public to the lobby of the Coral Gables Biltmore. (Santi Visalli/Coral Gables Biltmore)

The blue and starry groin vaults extend the length of the lobby. (Carol Berens)

An arcade overlooks the golf course and the lush courtyard restaurant below. The fountain and palm trees mark this romantic oasis. (Carol Berens)

The Governor Hotel's comfortable living-room lobby is warmed by the carpet and furniture's muted golds, burnt oranges, and greens, colors which complement the sepia tones of the four-paneled mural. The chandeliers are not original but recall the hotel's arts and crafts heritage, as does the exposed timber of the ceilings and walls.

(Governor Hotel)

In the Governor Hotel's lobby, a guest can write a letter under the greater than life-size murals of salmon fishing at Celilo Falls on the Columbia River. (Governor Hotel)

At the Jefferson in Richmond, Virginia, Thomas Jefferson is now surrounded by marble floors and carpet instead of the original alligator-filled moat. The carpet represents the areas that originally were grass. (© 1993 Prakash Patel/Jefferson Hotel)

Chapter 8

THE ATRIUM

People receive a spiritual release just watching the elevators fly up and down.[1]
John Portman

AT ITS BEST, the atrium hotel is hotel as entertainment, an elevator ride to the future. Hong Kong has wholeheartedly embraced this form at its most modern and extreme. John Portman, the Atlanta-based architect who has made atrium hotels his trademark, has been their main proponent in America. Two of the better atrium hotels are in his home town.

At its worst, the atrium hotel represents the antipathy of an urban hotel experience that is based on the interaction and sensual comfort of its guests. A city location does not automatically confer an urban character upon a hotel, a situation proven by those megastructures whose blank walls and parking lots act as fortresses shunning the city outside and impeding access to the lobby inside (see Chapter 2). Some large atrium hotels, such as the Marriott Marquis in New York and the Westin Bonaventure in Los Angeles, weave confusion and alienation into their design. Once inside the lobby, many floors above the sidewalk, social interaction is not spotlighted but is instead overshadowed by the hotel's own presence.

In its apparent intent to entertain, the atrium lobby risks merely overwhelming its guests, with success determined by how many gasps can be elicited. Visitors are expected to be impressed by its enormity and awed by the specialty of the hotel adventure. It is design as spectacle.

Through its command of technological virtuosity, the atrium lobby now often veers into science fiction excess. Its imagery exploits the gigantic and the infinite to create a vision of a future in which people are small and insignificant. Perhaps because of this, atrium-lobby hotels have become more suited for conventions while the more upscale hotels' public rooms tend to be smaller in scale and more personal.

Atlanta's Marriott Marquis Hotel is John Portman's extravagant expedition into science fiction and has been compared to moving within the ribcage of a whale. Its atrium's organic form enlivens the total volume, all the way up to the top.

(Atlanta Marriott)

Ironically, after spending all the money and effort to create a breathtaking multistory interior space, more money and greater effort are then spent to define the anonymous space on the lobby floor where the people are. Trailing ivy, swagging cloths, and imposing light fixtures are feeble attempts to create a warm, human-scaled interior space. They only serve to draw attention to the fact that these efforts are needed at all.

Atrium hotels most likely developed when exterior vehicular courtyards were roofed over with large skylights. Rising the full height of the building, the inner court became a bright room, ambiguously belonging to both the inside and outside, yet protected from the elements and bathed in daylight.

The 1873 San Francisco Palace Hotel is usually cited as one of the first atrium buildings. A center of social life in the West, the hotel's Great Court was a skylit vehicular courtyard. Carriages actually entered the building under the watchful eyes of the socially alert who would observe the court's comings and goings from the balconies of the seven stories above or from the garden on the ground floor. The importance of the Great Court was based on the activities of the people on the ground floor, not solely on the space above.

The vertical surfaces of the atrium are visually active. The clear articulation of each floor along with multiple columns and details enliven the atrium and provide a sense of scale: Columns with definite bases sit on balustrades; an arcade gracefully supports the structure overhead while separating the court from the hotel's other public rooms; and a syncopated pattern of columns adds interest to the wall plane. The difference between indoor and outdoor is indistinct; these interior atrium walls appear to be street facades, complete with street lights on the balconies.

Another pioneer atrium hotel is Denver's Brown Palace Hotel designed by Frank E. Edbrooke for Henry Brown, a silver miner who struck it rich. Opened in 1892, the Brown Palace was where prospectors paraded their recently unearthed wealth. Needless to say, the hotel's materials and architecture were designed to compete with this new-found prosperity and to represent the epitome of western luxury. Its eight-storied lobby is capped by a stained-glass domed skylight. This atrium is an impressive, unambiguous interior space. Although well lit from the outside, no carriages can enter its lobby, and its walls do not masquerade as building facades.

The designer justified the atrium's dramatic form because it provided cross-ventilation for guest rooms in pre-air-conditioned times. Mindful of every hotel owner's fear of fire, wood was only used in small details such as baseboards and moldings. The masonry construction was sheathed in the most luxurious of stones: red granite and sandstone on the exterior; marble and onyx on the interior.

The solid square columns at the base support elliptical arches, visually holding up the building. The upper stories turn into a scrim of classically detailed steel columns and ornate copper-plated railings. Although the atrium itself is impressive, the design and sumptuousness of the ground floor consciously engage the eye, enlivening the lobby area. Otherwise, attention would consistently be drawn to height and skylight above. The balcony railings serve as a uniform background, not upstaging the atrium or the lobby below.

One hundred years after the Brown Palace Hotel gave gold diggers a place to show off, the atrium hotel has come into its own. John Portman revived and expanded the form. His hotels exist primarily for their atriums. All other functions and aesthetics serve this master. His major invention was the exposed glass-caged elevator which, gliding through the vertical space, allows people to penetrate the full volume and height of the lobby.

Portman's first atrium hotel, the 1967 Atlanta Regency Hyatt, was a milestone in hotel design. At 23 stories high, its atrium has all the hallmarks that define his hotels. The hotel is chock-full of visual activity animating the atrium: The exposed elevators are transformed into moving, inhabitable sculptures; balconies overlook the lobby; interior planting proliferates; and large-scale sculptures fill the space. The elevators are as much a part of the public space as the lounges and bars on the lobby floor. Not only are they one of the major moving objects within the lobby, but they are also another way to see the lobby. They link the two major public areas: the revolving rooftop restaurant and the lobby below. The elevators are an event, like a special ride at an amusement park.

The San Francisco Hyatt Regency is another early entry in Portman's portfolio. Conceived as an integral part of the redevelopment of the Embarcadero Center, this hotel opened to popular and critical acclaim in 1973. The lobby floor, located on the second level atop large function rooms, is reached by escalators and experienced, not gradually, but all at once upon arrival. In plan and section, the hotel is a triangle with its north side sloping at a 45° angle that induces a feeling of being on the inside of a lopsided ziggurat. Although one of his simplest hotels, much visual animation emanates from the exposed elevators, the swirling-patterned tile, and many changing floor levels.

The San Francisco Hyatt Regency recently underwent an extensive renovation. The main goal of the renovation architects and interior designers (ELS/Elbasani & Logan Architects and Hirsch-Bedner & Associates, respectively) was to open up the space visually and physically to improve the hotel's relationship with the city. To this end, the street entrance was redesigned to produce a light-filled arcade. The demolition of the Embarcadero Freeway enabled some seating areas to have views out to the waterfront.

One of the unfortunate consequences of the sloping, terraced wall was the minimization of the skylight area, making the interior of the atrium extremely dark and the wall oppressive rather than uplifting. Now, vertical surfaces are lit to mimic daylight, washing the walls with warmth.

The atrium hotel has become a hotel style recognized around the world. Although not enamored of all, these hotels remind us of the fantastic, of our ability to be awed. These hotels have lived up to Portman's intentions, which he described when the Atlanta Regency Hyatt opened:

I wanted to explode the hotel; to open it up, to create a grandeur of space, almost a resort, in the center of the city. The whole idea was to open everything up; take the hotel from its closed, tight position and explode it; take the elevators and literally pull them out of the walls and let them become an experience within themselves, let them become a giant kinetic sculpture.[2]

(Above, left) The skylit courtyard of San Francisco's Palace Hotel: The hotel was destroyed in the 1906 fire that followed the earthquake and replaced with the present Sheraton Palace building. The ground floor of the court was an active place, accomodating carriages, people and, of course, the ubiquitous palms. Observers looked on the activity from behind the arcade or from the balcony corridors above. (Culver Pictures, Inc.)

(Above, right) Denver's Brown Palace Hotel: The rich onyx walls and cast-iron balconies express the lavishness of one of the first atrium hotels. The open railings on the galleries leading to guest rooms allowed the ground floor bartender to keep an eye on goings on upstairs. (Brown Palace Hotel)

(Right) The Hyatt Regency at Atlanta is Portman's first atrium hotel. The major design hallmarks of his atriums are evident here, such as the exposed glass elevators moving through the space, the large-scale sculptures, and plantings. (© Ron Rizzo/Creative Sources/Hyatt Regency)

(Left) Trees, planters, carpets, and comfortable seating help adapt the atrium's large space to a comfortable, livable scale. (ELS/Elbasani & Logan Architects/John Sutton ©)

(Below) The scale of the atrium is tamed and softened in the restaurant. The trees, flowers, wood screens, and spotlit tables make this a comfortable, inviting room within the room.
(ELS/Elbasani & Logan Architects/John Sutton ©)

(Right) A bird's-eye view of the lobby of San Francisco's Hyatt Regency. The light falling on the vertical surfaces is from artificial sources designed to simulate the play of daylight from the skylight (if the skylight were larger and the sun always shined). The sculpture, curved tubes of gold-anodized aluminum, was designed by Charles O. Perry and is part of the original hotel. Its 40-ft height and its transparency impart the appropriate scale and feeling for this space. (ELS/Elbasani & Logan Architects/John Sutton ©)

(Overleaf) Hong Kong has embraced the atrium hotel. The Grand Hyatt's allusions are many—from an ocean liner to Busby Berkeley movies—but the results are all its own. This lobby is not for the fainthearted but for those who want to be overwhelmed or entertained. People can try to one-up it, but it would be hard.
(Grand Hyatt, Hong Kong)

Chapter 9

THE CONTINENTAL EXPERIENCE: PALACES FOR THE RICH

It looks to me exactly like home; I thought I was back in Compiègne or Fontainebleau.
Empress Eugénie, about Le Grand Hôtel, Paris, 1862

THE HOTEL may be an American invention, but it's the grand European hotel that sets design standards. While American and European hotel forms often resemble each other, their substance indeed differs. There are dramatic contrasts in heritage and pedigree between European hotels and their American counterparts. In Europe, the phrase "fit for a king" constitutes no hyperbole because, in contrast to American hotels, which were built as palaces for the people, continental hotels were designed as palaces for royalty.

European hotels, often converted palaces or villas, maintain their aura as exclusive refuges for the rich and royal. Given this genesis, many old-world hotels are private affairs. Their lobbies and public spaces are small and restrictive, with social activity occurring behind closed doors among a select few. One patronizes these hotels seeking privacy and entertainment among friends. Notable exceptions exist, however, in the form of larger, more admissive hotels that open their social stage to a broader audience.

Although they never evolved into the civic laboratories of the American hotels, European hotels nonetheless remain important sites of social ritual and design advances. Regal as these hotels and their clientele were, they could not forever remain aloof from the products and inventions of their times. The great nineteenth- and early twentieth-century advances of railroads, technological developments, and international exhibitions influenced the design and use of hotels in Europe just as in America, although often at a slower pace. The social strata into which this progress was introduced did not always embrace the new with the same American thirst and fervor; rather, they often greeted change with

(Sacher Hotel)

the "tsk tsking" of steadfast conservatives lamenting the erosion of their known world.

Vicki Baum's *Grand Hotel* epitomized the Europe that did frequent its hotels. Through all the personal sagas and all the public displays of private events, the hotel was the main character, the perfect stage (and metaphor) upon which all lives intersected. The ambiance of the grand hotel's public rooms and its image of elegance encompassed all the senses, especially the aural, as in this passage:

> *The music from the tea-room in the new building beat in syncopation from mirror to mirror along the walls…Here the jazz band from the tea-room encountered the violins from the Winter Garden, while mingled with them came the thin murmur of the illuminated fountain as it fell into its imitation Venetian basin, the ring of glasses on tables, the creaking of wicker chairs and, lastly, a soft rustle of furs and silks in which women were moving to and fro.*

In England and France, international exhibitions of the mid- and late nineteenth century exploited and extolled the virtues of industry and technology. From the 1851 London Crystal Palace through the 1855 Paris Palais de l'Industrie and on to the 1889 fair that featured Eiffel's tower, exhibitions lured foreign visitors and ideas, which in turn spurred hotel development to accommodate travelers and social events. As in America, these expositions influenced building styles and methods well after their doors closed. The most obvious examples were the huge skylit courtyards of the 1855 Hotel du Louvre and the 1862 Grand Hotel Inter-Continental, both designed by Alfred Armand, which echoed the glass and iron vaults of the exposition's main building.

In England, communication and greater social fluidity emerged with the introduction of rail service, which displaced horse-drawn coaches and inns. Because of the expense, travel by horse-drawn coaches and stays in their associated inns were available mainly to the wealthy. As the network of rails developed, railroad prices decreased and the larger public was able to participate. Rival railroad companies bought land in towns and, seeking supporting businesses, built hotels adjacent to their stations.

The grand European hotel, however, evolved from palaces that accommodated traveling royalty into places at which like-minded souls gathered and flaunted their social status. Patrons not of royalty or related nobility were among the very wealthy and aspiring bourgeoisie. Opulent and ostentatious design emulated aristocratic tastes and pursuits for both the socially secure and the arriviste. Hotels trumpeted their design excursions to an irretrievable past, romantic images of royal pedigree. The same was done in America; however, Europe's castles and chateaux were closer to home. Hotels referred to actual styles and buildings, their design vocabulary a common language.

European urban hotel design drew inspiration from two French sources. First was the *hôtel particulier,* or the private city home, of the Parisian aristocracy. This mansion was a solid, free-standing affair entered through a U-shaped front courtyard. These residences were the social stages and seats of power of the upper classes, the venues of grand dinners, receptions, and masked balls. Although these stately homes performed many public functions, their ultimate purpose was flaunting the power and influence of their owners. This form, synonymous with aristocrat-

ic ambiance and social events, quickly became a model of hotel elegance, physically easy to emulate. The role of the powerful master, however, was more difficult, if not impossible, to appropriate. At the hotel, the cost of the room includes treating a guest as royally as an owner. One can imagine being ruler of the realm, but all know the truth: This is a shared fiction.

The exhilarating social whirl of the 1890s in Paris, dubbed the Belle Epoque for its exuberant joie de vivre, bubbled over French borders. International in scope, this was an era of elegance combined with frivolous enjoyment, a decade when pursuit of upper class amusement was raised to a high art. It was a way of life not only for socialites but, for all its rigidity and rules, also open to writers, actors, and artists, if only for the amusement of the former.

Institutions became somewhat more accessible than the previous epochs of strict separation of classes and of private entertainment. Design goals ensured the luxury that royalty expected while combining more public spaces to accommodate the social and theatrical aspects of the high life. Hotels and their associated dining rooms were the venues of much public entertainment.

(Above) The scale of the Savoy's lobby reflects
the obvious public nature of the hotel.
(The Savoy)

(Left) The first wave of American influence
revolved around technological advances; the
second introduced the American bar.
Previously in Europe, social life took place in
restaurants; however, after World War I,
American expatriates (with Prohibition in
full swing back home) created a demand for
the bar. At the Savoy, the American Bar, a
small enclave hidden away upstairs, still fills
this role. Comfortable chairs and sofas are
scattered about to create conversation areas.
(The Savoy)

(Left; Carol Berens)

(Right) Echoing the arcades of Paris's rue de Rivoli and the Place Vendome, the London Ritz wholeheartedly embraces Piccadilly. Although bathed in tradition, the stone exterior of the London Ritz masks the fact that it was the first completely steel-framed building in London. Since technology outpaced building codes, the exterior walls were required to be built to bearing wall thickness. (London Ritz)

(Below) The rotunda vestibule greets guests and starts the wide, vaulted corridor which ends with the restaurant. The Savonnerie carpets of red and gold further direct the flow and are typical of the rich materials used throughout the Ritz. (London Ritz)

(Above) Unity of the design vision is epitomized by this room. Echoing the Palm Court, the bar is a smaller, slightly less formal room using the same features, such as chairs, paneled mirrors, and colors. (London Ritz)

(Left) The heart of the Ritz resides in the Palm Court, raised several steps above the main gallery and framed by two Ionic columns. One can have a good view of who is there and yet be slightly distant from the flow of people. It has become renowned for its afternoon teas. The Louis XVI decoration is in full bloom. The medallioned chairs, gilded garlands capping paneled beveled mirrors, and glass ceiling bespoke traditional luxury to the Edwardians for whom it was designed as well as for us today. (London Ritz)

At this same time, around the turn of the century, the Prince of Wales, the future King Edward VII, put his stamp on this era as surely as his mother, Queen Victoria, influenced hers. The Prince loved the good life. The Prince loved hotels. The Prince loved all things French. These pleasures stimulated a lively social whirl, with high society mingling with those in the arts.

In London, the relationship between theater and hotels was cemented in 1889 with the Savoy Hotel. Built by Richard D'Oyly Carte, the eponymous director of the Gilbert and Sullivan Opera Company, the hotel next to the Savoy Theatre on the Thames enticed and entertained royalty and actors. During the nineteenth century, most hotels in England were private inns and enclaves with small reception areas because guests usually dined in their rooms. Those dining rooms that did exist did not seat women. Not only did the Savoy end this tradition, it also successfully petitioned and changed the laws to permit dining rooms to open after theater hours.

At its opening, the Savoy's manager was Cesar Ritz; its chef, Escoffier; its musician, Johann Strauss. The hotel signaled the change of social setting from private houses to more public arenas. A success from the start, its most famous habitué was the Prince of Wales, along with Lily Langtry, Sarah Bernhardt, and a host of other royalty and stars.

Sparing no expense, D'Oyly Carte instructed his architect, T. E. Collcutt, to incorporate the latest American inventions, such as elevators, bathrooms, and fireproof construction, into his first-class establishment. Designed for entertainment, its public spaces expand throughout the ground floor. From the entry, inserted at the end of its own private road, the public areas cascade down toward the tearoom and restaurant overlooking the Thames. The lobby, reception, and various meeting places descend toward the river as well as fan out, each level progressively leading to embrace the view at the end.

The energies and visions of those who created the Savoy regrouped several years later with a Beaux-Arts-trained French Alsatian architect to create the epitome of the grand European hotel. Cesar Ritz, the Prince of Wales, and Charles Mewès captured the hotel spirit and defined the style of the continent at the turn of the century. In England, France, and Spain, their hotels represented the best throughout Europe and the world and influenced form and taste wherever they were located.

Cesar Ritz's London hotel was designed by Charles Mewès (also the architect of the Paris Ritz) along with another Beaux-Arts-trained British architect, Arthur J. Davis, in 1904. The London Ritz is a little bit of Paris dropped intact onto Piccadilly. From its mansard roof to its arcades reminiscent of the rue de Rivoli, the London Ritz majestically anchors its stretch of a central London street.

Its plan is simplicity itself; its public spaces are graciously presented to great advantage. Paralleling the street arcade outside, the lobby's grand procession starts with a circular vestibule and progresses through a gallery with alcoved, undulating walls, the restaurant its goal. Perpendicular to the main axis and at the end of a shorter axis is the heart of the hotel's public space, the Palm Court. Three steps elevate it above the main gallery and enhance this perfect setting at which to see and be seen.

The hotel's public role is unambiguous, from the arcades' embrace of the street to the grand procession of the interior. The ground floor, although not large, is concentrated in purpose and totally devoted to public spaces. Its decoration is unified. Mewès hearkened to a Louis XVI style to convey elegant simplicity as well as contrived formality.

One of the few extant examples of an Art Deco hotel in London is the Dorchester on Park Lane overlooking Hyde Park. Designed in 1931 by Sir Owen Williams and William Curtis Green, the Dorchester has recently been refurbished and polished to within an inch of its life. The public spaces, a simple entry foyer and a long, columned promenade, form a T. The decoration and ornament of the existing hotel derive from the contrast and luxury of its materials. The result is a formal but less traditional sense of elegance.

Art Deco also prevails at the Park Lane Hotel, which predates the Dorchester by four years. When it opened, each major gathering space was a study in a different culture or epoch—the Louis XIV Grill Room, Old English Breakfast Room, Tutor Smoke Room, and Old Roman Lobby Lounge—(but today in its public spaces, only its Art Deco nature and details survive. Epitomizing the elegant and sophisticated backdrop of the social scene of the years between the wars, the Park Lane Hotel plays itself on screen in productions such as *Brideshead Revisited* and *House of Elliot.*

England, perhaps, has perfected the more intimate form of the living-room lobby. Located in genteel, traditional hotels, these lobbies, or more likely tearooms, represent the archetype of the comfortable and cozy, yet impeccably detailed, city hotel disguised as a country house. One of the best is Brown's Hotel in Piccadilly. Begun as a small inn, over the years Brown's Hotel accumulated the surrounding buildings, its enlargement leading to the need for public rooms. Ostensibly simple, its public rooms exude the ease and naturalness of a country home, which is apparently difficult to achieve considering the poor imitations that abound.

Building by accretion created the same need, if not the same feel, for public rooms at Claridge's in Mayfair. Although it started as a series of small apartments, by the turn of the century, through physical and social expansion, it tried to rival the Ritz as the location for public rituals such as dining and balls. Its Georgian exterior has hosted many interior styles from the French, as influenced by the Ritz, to 1930s eclecticism, to the restrained traditional elegance of today.

Paris, a city of interior courtyards, hosts a number of exceptional hotels, almost all of which embrace courts at their centers. Whether a landscaped garden only for visual pleasure or an impeccably decorated restaurant for lunch or a starlit dinner, these courtyards define and organize the public spaces of Paris's grand hotels.

The Grand Hotel Inter-Continental emerged during the same era and with the same expansive spirit as Haussmann's Paris and Garnier's Opera. Located on

(Right) The Dorchester's black and white marble floor reflects the half dome of the rotunda ceiling. The entry is a simple statement leading slightly off axis toward the ornate promenade beyond. The decoration of the foyer derives more from the contrast of rich materials than from surface ornament. The promenade seems to be endless, an appearance at first attributed to mirrors, which as it turns out is not the case. (The Dorchester)

(Below) A more intimate look at the promenade, with comfortable, relaxed seating (compare these poufs with the ones at the Willard Inter-Continental; Chapter 5). Cool greens contrast nicely with gold, maintaining the lightness of the room. In an extremely axial room, all furnishings and details are round and soft. (The Dorchester)

(Far right) The Dorchester's long promenade achieves a comfortable scale through the segmentation of furniture arrangements which are reinforced by segmented ceilings. The materials remain rich and luxurious throughout. The yellow marble columns and pilasters sport gilded Ionic capitals to ensure that all sparkles. The light golden glow of the room exudes gaiety not staidness. The furniture, however, appears to be out of sync with its Art Deco heritage. (The Dorchester)

(Above) The fanlike column capitals, coved ceiling, lit railings, and air vents are classic Art Deco details in the Park Lane Hotel's Silver Gallery Entrance, which leads to banqueting functions. (Park Lane Hotel)

(Left) The Palm Court Lounge's arched, skylit ceiling is the defining characteristic of the room. Opening directly onto the foyer, it was originally the lobby lounge, with living-room groupings of furniture. The setting has become a bit more formal for afternoon tea.
(Park Lane Hotel)

(Right) Wood paneling, molded ceilings, elaborate cornices, soft carpeted corridors, soft colors, and lots of chintz reinforce the living-room feel of Brown's tearoom. All is seamless: Even the fresh flowers complement the decor. What better place could one imagine for having tea on a gray afternoon? (Brown's Hotel)

(Left, above) Looking down from the stair landing, Claridge's front hall with its signature black and white patterned marble floors sets the tone of refined elegance that pervades the hotel. The light colors are welcoming, and details such as the arches and molding are subtly defined. The front hall literally sparkles without being ostentatious or gaudy. (Leading Hotels of the World)

(Left, bottom) On the other side of the arches, tradition seeps into every detail of Claridge's foyer. (Leading Hotels of the World)

(Above) At London's Edwardian era Hyde Park Hotel, ornamentation is achieved by the contrasting colors of rich materials. Eight different types of marble, under years of paint, wallpaper, and wood paneling, were uncovered during a recent renovation. (Hyde Park Hotel)

the Place de l'Opéra and home to the Cafe de la Paix, the Grand Hotel's history parallels its times, its fortunes rising and falling with the rhythm of politics as well as with its ability to remain abreast of technological advances and stylistic sensibilities.

In the 1860s, its courtyard served as the traditional Parisian vehicular (horse-drawn carriage) entrance but, being glazed over, is also comparable to San Francisco's Sheraton Palace Hotel. At the turn of the century, the advent of the automobile rendered this use of the court obsolete. The entry was moved around the corner, and the courtyard was transformed from the reception area into a winter garden featuring a tea salon and restaurant. Over the years, this courtyard mirrored the tastes of the times. Recently, 1970s modern decor was peeled away to reveal original Second Empire moldings and detail. Redesigned to connect with a spacious, bright entry, the glazed courtyard now is the visual as well as functional center of its public spaces.

The courtyard adapts to any mood as can be seen by comparing the exuberant declaration of iron technology of Le Grand Hôtel Inter-Continental to the sedate, superbly manicured French garden of Le Bristol. Le Bristol, although opened in 1924, communicates the refined elegance of the eighteenth century. Catering to heads of state and business rather than the actors and personalities of the more brash palace hotels, Le Bristol projects the cool, quiet feeling of a private enclave. While its art and furnishings hearken to France's place in history, the open plan and clean lines recall its more modern heritage. Its public areas flow into one another, from its open lobby through to the bar and various seating areas culminating at its prized center, the restful garden.

Not all hotels in Paris hearken to its irretrievable royal past. Nestled within its intricate fabric, Paris overflows with small, intimate hotels, usually inconspicuous private retreats. The Hotel Montalembert, located on a quiet street in the heart of the Left Bank, is that hotel rarity: unabashedly modern, yet warm and inviting; small, yet accessible to the public. Its 1926 structure has been recently renovated according to designs of Christian Liaigre.

The openness of the Montalembert's public areas is immediately perceived from the street. Arched ground floor windows act as storefronts, inviting passers-by as well as bringing light into the interior during daytime. During the summer, tables with umbrellas form an outdoor cafe, further advertising the hotel's presence. The lobby, seating areas, restaurant, and bar all flow into each other, with furniture arrangements creating functional distinctions. For all its modernity, the hotel performs as a comfortable, traditional living room.

The early 1900s saw the building of two grand hotels on an international scale in Madrid. Conscious that his capital was far from the playgrounds of European royalty and wanting to remedy the lack of local places for the pleasures of the aristocracy, King Alfonso XIII of Spain encouraged first building the Hotel Ritz in 1910 and then, in 1913, the Palace Hotel. Both are in the heart of Madrid, amid the Museo del Prado, Museo Thyssen, and major parks.

For the Hotel Ritz in Madrid, the architect Charles Mewès reprised his seemingly mistake-proof formula for summoning up classical French styles as symbols of luxury and elegance. Begun as a franchise from Cesar Ritz, the Madrid hotel enjoyed its exclusive role as surely as its siblings around the world played theirs. Although molded from stucco rather than etched in stone, the facade's garlands, ribbons, and keystones with modeled heads trumpet the formal settings within.

An exuberant symbol of the Belle Epoque, the Ritz's neighbor, the Palace Hotel, has 500 rooms and is large by European luxury hotel standards. The building plan is trapezoidal, occupying an entire city block. In its center, both physically and psychically, is the magnificent rotunda lobby, capped by a spectacular stained-glass dome. This rotunda has been the meeting place for artists, politicians, and celebrities. An active participant in the life of its city, it's hard to believe that the rotunda was an operating room during the Spanish Civil War when the Palace Hotel was turned into a hospital.

Not all European hotels seek their style from French royalty as the Hotel Alfonso XIII in Seville can testify. Built to accommodate the Ibero-American Exhibition of 1929, the hotel is just a few steps from Seville's famous Giralda Tower (the inspiration for the Coral Gables Biltmore). The Hotel Alfonso XIII reflects its city's 500 years of Arab influence as well as the Edwardian eclecticism of its times. Although it reflects centuries of tradition and culture, the hotel did not evolve; it was created: a stage set that actually relates, if only as hyperbole, to its surroundings. Recently renovated for Expo 92, the hotel describes itself as a showcase of Moorish revival, Spanish Renaissance, and Andalusian baroque. The Art Deco craze of its era seems to have passed it by.

The extravagance and scale of the building are reflected in its public spaces. The plan of the hotel is axial, creating a linear progression from the entrance, to the lobby, and through to a large central exterior patio. Every opening is arched; every surface ripe with ornament and detail. The extensive use of tile and geometric patterns refers to the Moslem influence in the region; its modern conveniences relate to the western elite clientele.

The competition among European capitals for first-rate, deluxe hotels was fierce. It was a contest that Rome, newly named as capital, could not resist. It, too, had to have its Ritz. Thus, in 1894, the Grand Hotel was built near the Baths of Diocletian by the Ritz hotel group, the Foreign and London Grand Hotel Syndicate. Designed by the Italian architect Cavalier Podesti, the interiors were completed by Madame Ritz herself. Soon local society women were seen in its public rooms, and the winter-weary Savoy crowd frequented its cousin in warmer, sunnier Rome. A hotel this central to the pulse of its city becomes linked to its events. Thus, the Grand Hotel, home to traveling royalty, was also home to Mussolini and important Axis members as well as to various liberation forces at the end of the war.

Situated atop the Spanish Steps in the heart of Rome, the Hotel Hassler represents quiet elegance. Through a novel interpretation of providing the most up-to-date conveniences with the feeling of history, the Hotel Hassler was totally rebuilt after the war, its facade historically re-created. Taking advantage of its geographical prominence, its rooftop garden overlooks some of the best known Roman monuments such as St. Peter's Dome and the Pantheon.

(Above) Contrasting with the wide open spaces and bright sunlight of La Verriere, the bar is a picture of English clubbiness. With its mahogany paneling, brass fittings, and plush red carpet, it is a warm, welcoming, and quiet retreat. (Le Grand Hotel)

(Left) Recently renovated, the central courtyard of Le Grand Hotel Inter-Continental, now called La Verriere, reprises the 1907 winter garden on a scale reminiscent of a town square. All the hotel's public space flows toward the lightness and openness of this room. Recalling the ironwork by Eiffel and the great expositions that influenced the era of the hotel's beginnings, the huge skylight once again shelters a tea salon and restaurant. (Le Grand Hotel)

(Left, above) The Hotel Le Bristol is quiet and refined. The Carrara marble floor, Savonnerie carpet, and Baccarat crystal chandeliers, as well as fine art and antiques, are immediately perceived upon entry. The lightness and openness of the entrance's clean lines avoid the stuffiness that is so often the demise of this style.
(Karen Weiner Escalera Associates)

(Left, below) This vignette sums up the hotel's essence. The Flemish tapestry behind the cozy seating area shows how attention has been given to every detail. The wrought-iron banister provides lightness and ornament.
(Karen Weiner Escalera Associates)

(Above) In the ultimate gesture of elegance, even the wood-paneled bar possesses period furniture, crystal chandeliers, and tapestries.
(Karen Weiner Escalera Associates)

(Left) It's hard to believe that the pulse of the city beats just feet away from this quiet retreat. Although a formal French garden, the building's colonnade and arches lend it scale and intimacy. (Karen Weiner Escalera Associates)

*(Left and above) Presenting a more
unrestrained interpretation of the outdoor
room, the Hôtel Plaza Athénée's red awnings
and umbrellas lend gaiety to the garden court.
(M. Smith/Hôtel Plaza-Athénée)*

*(Above) The gallery around the garden court
is set up for tea and cocktails.
(Hôtel Plaza-Athénée)*

(Above) The frosted glass canopy of the Hôtel Montalembert entrance. (Hôtel Montalembert)

(Right) Simplicity and warmth mark the entry of the hotel. The ebony framed openings give structure to the space while the various neutral creams, beiges, and browns convey a feeling of refined luxury. The carpet, which claims to be a reproduction of Count de Montalembert's handwriting, adds texture and direction to the room while grounding the design in history. The restaurant continues the color scheme through the use of wood paneling, black framed chairs, and black and white photographs. Throughout, all details are attended to, including the site-specific wrought-iron ashtray in the corner.

(Hôtel Montalembert)

(Above, left) The combination of traditional furniture with modern details can be seen in the restaurant-cafe. (Hôtel Montalembert)

(Above) The whimsy of the details can be seen in this stair-railing detail. The golden square pattern of the wall is typical of the restrained decoration that is the hallmark of this design. (Hôtel Montalembert)

(Left) Located between the restaurant and the garden court, the library-seating-bar area is made more inviting during the gray winter with a roaring fire. The color scheme with the additional golds and reds of the carpet and upholstery complements the room, bringing out the warmth of the wood paneling. (Hôtel Montalembert)

(Above) The circular upper hall embodies the formal tradition that is the hallmark of the Madrid Ritz. The cream colors, marble floors, and the handcrafted carpet made specifically for this room work together to define the hotel. The gilded carvings of the mirror and table are typical of its design era.
(Hotel Ritz Madrid)

(Right) Diana the Huntress in her niche watches as the powerful have their morning coffee or afternoon tea amid the carved garlands, oculi, and balustrades.
(Hotel Ritz Madrid)

(Below) The Madrid Ritz's terrace is a cool oasis overlooking the formal landscaped gardens beyond. The curved stairs stepping down into the garden are the perfect stage for making an entrance. (Hotel Ritz Madrid)

(Above) This is where Jake and Lady Brett had goodbye drinks in The Sun Also Rises *and where modern day politicians exchange the news of the day. The warm neutral colors bathe the room in an understated elegance and calm; people provide the color and activity. (Palace Hotel-Madrid)*

(Left) Ernest Hemingway, Pablo Picasso, Salvador Dali, and Mata Hari all were drawn to the drama of the Palace Hotel's Rotunda, whose central location and exuberant skylit dome make this a prime meeting space in Madrid. Although the space could be overwhelming, intricate carvings and patterns introduce a smaller, more intimate scale to the room. Living-room lamps and furniture arrangements further reinforce the comfort of the room.
(Palace Hotel-Madrid)

(Overleaf) The entrance to the Hotel Alfonso XIII interprets the local Moorish and Andalusian traditions on a public and theatrical scale. (Hotel Alfonso XIII)

(Page 175) The Hotel Alfonso XIII's courtyard was designed for pre-air-conditioned times, although today it remains a visual delight. (Hotel Alfonso XIII)

(Left) Two views of the grand salon at the
Grand Hotel, Rome. (Le Grand Hotel-Rome)

(Below) The bar at the Grand Hotel, Rome.
(Le Grand Hotel-Rome)

(Above, left) The lobby of the Hotel Hassler.
(Lou Hammond & Associates)

(Above, right) The rooftop restaurant of the
Hotel Hassler takes advantage of its
prominent location at the top of the Spanish
Steps. (Lou Hammond & Associates)

(Right) The garden cafe of the Hotel Hassler.
(Lou Hammond & Associates)

(Above) Shepheard's Hotel in Cairo, Egypt, epitomized a protected and popular seat from which to view local culture. Foreign activity in Cairo centered on the hotel's terrace, raised several steps above the street. Shepheard's terrace was an inverted stage: Members of the audience (that is, travelers) safely watched the tumult and excitement of the Arab market at their feet with no obligation to involve themselves in the action. It so captured the imagination of western travelers that many considered it a "combination of Paris and Saratoga."[1] This, however, was interactive theater. The local populace, conversely, became an audience observing (also from a safe distance) visitors on the terrace. An ostentatious symbol of foreign presence, Shepheard's was burned down during anticolonist riots in 1951. (Culver Pictures)

(Above) The dense, ornate atmosphere of the Pera Palas Hotel interior emanates from the nature of the materials themselves as well as from surface decoration, furnishings, and plants. The colorful, veined green marble of the columns contrasting with the patterned and bordered rose of the walls animates the lobby. Further layering of detail is achieved through the muntins of the windows beyond, recalling simultaneously the domes of Turkish mosques and Gothic spires (a favorite Victorian reference). (Hotel Pera Palas)

(Left) This period photo of the present-day Agatha Christie Room conjures up exotic assignations involving romance, espionage, and international diplomacy. It's easy to imagine Mata Hari or Ataturk sauntering in. No surface is left untouched. The variegated, striped marble walls and the flowered, dark oriental carpets strewn about divert the eye, preventing any singular focus.
(Hotel Pera Palas)

(Above) Agatha Christie's several stays at the hotel inspired the naming of this room (and perhaps her book Murder on the Orient Express). Modern sensibilities have lightened and simplified the room; however, the innate decoration of the materials still predominates. A voluminous room, the totally different treatment of the first and second stories intensifies the ornate, somewhat fussy, character. (Hotel Pera Palas)

(Left) A model of simplicity compared to the rest of the hotel, the Orient Express Bar's comfortable seating encourages small conversational groups while accommodating some stools at the bar. Ironically, with its large arched windows, the bar is more open than other hotel public areas and is a bright and open room for daytime use. (Hotel Pera Palas)

(Right) The original lobby of the Manila Hotel evokes the turn-of-the-century tropics. An easy entente with heat-induced torpor is suggested by the arched openings, palms, and light wicker furniture. The lobby, situated at the main entrance overlooking the park, maximized not only bay breezes but also social exhibition and observation. Western forms were adapted to the tropics. William Parsons, the official American architect of the Philippines, extended openings to the floor and used canopies and arcades to protect guests from sun and glare while maintaining ventilation. In his quest for permanent building materials, Parsons encouraged the use of reinforced concrete as a construction standard. (Architectural Record and Avery Architecture and Fine Arts Library, Columbia University)

(Left, bottom) The Manila's huge lobby, created in the 1970s, links the original lobby, which is now an entry way, to the new annex. Although the larger scale changes the intimacy of the room, the white arcaded walls echo the spirit of the old. The interior finishings compose a virtual encyclopedia of Philippine materials and craft work: decorative narra wood coffered ceilings, inlaid marble floors, and seashell chandeliers.
(Manila Hotel)

(Left) The lobby of the Oriental in Bangkok combines traditional Thai images and costumes with the new. (The Oriental Bangkok)

(Below) The Oriental's outdoor Authors' Lounge is named after the long tradition of western writers finding refuge at the hotel.
(Leading Hotels of the World)

The Western Refuge 189

(Above) All coolness and elegance, the Mandarin Oriental Hotel's main lobby combines fine materials and rich colors. The many levels create great people-watching vantages as well as different gathering places. The lobby is large without overwhelming guests with its importance.
(Lou Hammond & Associates)

(Right) The east lobby continues the black marble and gold color combinations.
(Leading Hotels of the World)

(Below) The gold and Chinese motifs enliven the rather formal setting of the Mandarin Hotel's Captain's Bar, though the sofas stress comfort. This is a place for business rather than an intimate tête-à-tête.
(Leading Hotels of the World)

(Right) Built in 1928, the Peninsula Hotel is Hong Kong's grande dame and a glorious reminder of the heyday of Hong Kong's expatriate community.
(The Peninsula/Murphy.O'Brien Communications)

(Below) Afternoon tea, a socially defining custom, is served in the lobby.
(The Peninsula/Murphy.O'Brien Communications)

(Inset) Close-up of the elaborate detail of the Peninsula's ceiling.
(The Peninsula/Murphy.O'Brien Communications)

(Overleaf) The view looking at Hong Kong island from its magnificent setting on the Kowloon side on the bay permeates the Regent's lobby. Modern, slick details of floor-to-ceiling window walls and highly reflective finishes dissolve in the background to enhance and burnish the spectacular view. The sitting arrangement is obvious, but would anyone want to be anywhere else?
(The Regent, Hong Kong)

(Left) Lobby of the Kowloon Shangri-La Hotel. (M. Darby/Shangri-la Hotels)

(Below) Lobby of the Island Shangri-La Hotel, Hong Kong. (M. Darby/Shangri-la Hotels)

(Right) A quiet retreat from the Island Shangri-La's active lobby, this room combines high volume, rich materials, and European allusions to create its own interpretation of a club room. The long, narrow proportion of the room encourages an intimate feeling. The large sun-streamed windows dispel the usual interiorness of a club. For the evening, the table lamps create a soft atmosphere that just recessed spotlights cannot. (M. Darby/Shangri-la Hotels)

FURTHER READING

Arnold, Wendy. *The Historic Hotels of London, A Select Guide.* New York: Holt, Rinehart and Winston, 1986.

Arnold, Wendy. *Historic Hotels of Paris, A Select Guide.* San Francisco: Chronicle Books, 1990.

Breeze, Carla. *Pueble Deco.* New York: Rizzoli International Publications, 1990.

Cerwinske, Laura. *Tropical Deco: The Architecture and Design of Old Miami Beach.* New York: Rizzoli International Publications, Inc., 1980.

Donzel, Catherine, Gregory, Alexis, and Walter, Marc. *Grand American Hotels.* New York: Vendome Press, 1989.

End, Henry. *Interiors Book of Hotels and Motor Hotels.* New York: Whitney Library of Design, 1963.

Frischauer, Willi. *The Grand Hotels of Europe.* New York: Coward-McCann, Inc., 1965.

Grimes, William. *Straight Up or on the Rocks: A Cultural History of American Drink.* New York: Simon and Schuster, 1993.

Hatton, Hap. *Tropical Splendor, An Architectural History of Florida.* New York: Alfred A. Knopf, 1987.

Lapidus, Morris. *An Architecture of Joy.* Miami: E. A. Seemann, 1977.

Limerick, Jeffrey, Ferguson, Nancy, and Oliver, Richard. *America's Grand Resort Hotels.* New York: Pantheon Books, 1979

Lowe, David. *Chicago Interiors, Views of a Splendid World.* Chicago: Contemporary Books, 1979.

Lowe, David. *Lost Chicago.* New York: Americana Legacy Press, 1985, © 1975 (distributed by Crown Publishers).

Ludy, R. B. *Historic Hotels of the World.* Philadelphia: David McKay Co., 1927.

Mathew, Christopher. *A Different World, Stories of Great Hotels.* New York and London: Paddington Press Ltd., 1976.

Meade, Martin. *Grand Oriental Hotels from Cairo to Tokyo, 1800–1939.* New York: Vendome Press, 1987 (distributed by Rizzoli International Publications, Inc.).

Olson, Arlene. *A Guide to the Architecture of Miami Beach.* Miami: Dade Heritage Trust, 1978.

Pevsner, Nikolaus. *History of Building Types.* Princeton: Princeton University Press, 1976.

Stern, Robert A. M., Gilmartin, Gregory, and Mellens, Thomas R. *New York 1930, Architecture and Urbanism Between the Two World Wars.* New York: Rizzoli International Publications, Inc., 1987.

Stern, Robert A. M., Gilmartin, Gregory, and Massengate, J. *New York 1900.* New York: Rizzoli International Publications, Inc., 1983.

Watkin, David. *Grand Hotel: Golden Age of Palace Hotels.* New York: Vendome Press, 1984.

White, Arthur. *Palaces of the People, A Social History of Commercial Hospitality.* New York: Toplinger Publishing Co., 1970.

Wiffen, Marcus. *Pueblo Deco: The Art Deco Architecture of the Southwest.* Albuquerque: University of New Mexico Press, 1984.

Williamson, Jefferson. *The American Hotel.* New York: Arno Press, 1975 (orig. 1930).

FOOTNOTES

CHAPTER ONE

[1]A.C. David, "Three New Hotels," *The Architectural Record* 18 (March 1905): 185.

[2]John W. Cook and Heinrich Klotz, Conversations with Architects (New York: Praeger, 1973), p.156.

CHAPTER TWO

[1]John W. Cook and Heinrich Klotz, Conversations with Architects (New York: Praeger, 1973), p.157.

CHAPTER THREE

[1]Sarmiento, Domingo Faustino, Irving A. Leonard, translator. *Abroad in America: Visitors to the New Nation 1776–1914,* edited by Marc Pachter. (Reading, MA: Addison-Wesley Publishing Co. and National Portrait Gallery, Smithsonian Institution, 1976.)

[2]For a literary analysis of the use and image of hotels in Edith Wharton's novels, see Susan Koprince's essay, "Edith Wharton's Hotels" in *Massachusetts Studies in English.* 1985, Vol. 10, pp. 12–23.

[3]Williamson, Jefferson. *The American Hotel* [New York: Arno Press, 1975 (orig. 1930).]

[4]Ludy, R. B. *Historic Hotels of the World.* (Philadelphia: David McKay Co., 1927).

CHAPTER FIVE

[1]Five years later, these architects would design the Sheraton Palace Hotel in San Francisco.

[2]Arthur C. David, "The St. Regis—The Best Type of Metropolitan Hotel," *The Architectural Record* Vol. 15 (June 1904): 553.

[3]Williamson, Jefferson. *The American Hotel* [New York: Arno Press, 1975 (orig. 1930).]

[4]This process has recently been revived for the wall art at the 1992 Four Seasons Hotel in New York.

[5]For an excellent survey and discussion of these hotels, see *America's Grand Resort Hotels* by Jeffrey Limerick, Nancy Ferguson, and Richard Oliver (New York: Pantheon Books, 1979)

CHAPTER SIX

[1]Interiors were also designed by Rita St. Clair & Associates (public spaces) and Ellen McCluskey.

[2]This city-within-a-city design features some of the urban design concepts put forth in the early 1920s by planners. Traffic and parking problems were tackled by separating pedestrian and vehicular circulation systems. Pedestrian bridges span roadways and connect office buildings to shopping arcades on upper floors while parking is located in separate garages. Rockefeller Center, another Art Deco masterpiece built several years after the Cincinnati complex, derives from a similar concept, minus the skywalks.

[3]The Arizona Biltmore's official architect is Albert Chase McArthur. Frank Lloyd Wright is listed as consulting architect. McArthur was a student of Wright's and, more important, was a member of the family who built the hotel in 1929. Because much of the plan, details, and feel of the hotel recall Frank Lloyd Wright, McArthur's claim has been challenged by some.

CHAPTER EIGHT

[1]*New York Times,* October 12, 1985.

[2]John Portman and Jonathan Barnett, *The Architect as Developer* (New York: McGraw-Hill, 1976).

CHAPTER TEN

[1]Ludy, R. B. *Historic Hotels of the World,* Philadelphia: David McKay Co., 1927.

MCNY–Museum of The City of New York.

INDEX

About the Author

Carol Berens, an architect and writer, is currently a vice president at the Empire State Development Corporation in New York City.